In cooperation with

NorthStar

Building Skills for the TOEFL® iBT

Intermediate

TEACHER'S MANUAL

with

ETS® SCORING GUIDE

John Beaumont

Series Editors
Frances Boyd
Carol Numrich

PEARSON
Longman

NorthStar: Building Skills for the TOEFL iBT Teacher's Manual Intermediate

Pearson Education, 10 Bank Street, White Plains, NY 10606

Staff credits: The people who made up the **NorthStar: Building Skills for the TOEFL iBT Intermediate Teacher's Manual** team, representing editorial, production, design, and manufacturing, are Dave Dickey, Melissa Leyva, Sherry Preiss, Robert Ruvo, Barbara Sabella, Debbie Sistino, and Paula Van Ells.

The ETS® Scoring Guide was written by the ETS staff.

Text composition: TSI Graphics
Text font: Sabon

LONGMAN ON THE **WEB**

Longman.com offers online resources for teachers and students. Access our Companion Websites, our online catalog, and our local offices around the world.

Visit us at **longman.com**.

ISBN: 0-13-188565-0

Printed in the United States of America
1 2 3 4 5 6 7 8 9 10–ML–11 10 09 08 07 06

Contents

Scope and Sequence
for NorthStar: Building Skills for the TOEFL iBT Intermediate Student Book

Unit	Listening	Reading
1 **Advertising**	**Campus Conversation:** Listen to a student and a professor talk about false advertising. **Academic Listening:** Listen to radio ads.	**Essay:** Read about advertising in world markets.
2 **Extreme Sports**	**Campus Conversation:** Listen to a student and a professor talk about parents' expectations. **Academic Listening:** Listen to a lecture about the personality of an extreme-sport athlete.	**Newspaper Article:** Read about an athlete's eating disorder.
3 **Fraud**	**Campus Conversation:** Listen to a student and a financial aid advisor talk about scholarships. **Academic Listening:** Listen to statements made by victims of fraud.	**Advertisement:** Read about an alternative health center.
4 **Storytelling**	**Campus Conversation:** Listen to a student and a professor talk about making an oral presentation. **Academic Listening:** Listen to an interview with storyteller Jackie Torrence.	**Review:** Read about the short story "The Metamorphosis."
5 **Language**	**Campus Conversation:** Listen to a student and a resident assistant talk about living and communicating in a new place. **Academic Listening:** Listen to an interview about gender and language.	**Magazine Article:** Read about code switching, or switching between languages while speaking.

Speaking	Writing	Skill Focus
Integrated Task: 1. Read about different advertising techniques. 2. Listen to a lecture about emotional appeals in ads. 3. Speak about emotional appeals in advertising.	**Independent Task:** Write about a product you like, and how to advertise it.	**Skimming and Scanning:** Learn how to find information quickly.
Independent Task: Speak about a time when you did something obsessively (sports, music, games, etc.).	**Integrated Task:** 1. Read the definitions of *obsession*. 2. Listen to an interview with a skateboarder. 3. Write about which definition fits the skateboarder's experience.	**Making Inferences:** Learn how to make guesses about information not stated directly.
Integrated Task: 1. Read about "quacks," or people who offer miracle cures. 2. Listen to an excerpt about a patient who went to a quack. 3. Speak about the reasons for and against going to a quack.	**Independent Task:** Write about an experience you have had with fraud or dishonesty.	**Using Context Clues:** Learn how to use surrounding information to understand meaning, details, and inferences.
Independent Task: Tell a short story in which you or someone you know is an animal, plant, or other nonhuman thing.	**Integrated Task:** 1. Read about anthropomorphism. 2. Listen to an excerpt from "The Metamorphosis." 3. Write about how the author of "The Metamorphosis" uses anthropomorphism.	**Identifying and Using Rhetorical Structure:** Learn how to recognize and use rhetorical structures in a whole written or spoken passage or part of one.
Integrated Task: 1. Read about stereotyping. 2. Listen to an interview with someone who was stereotyped because of his accent. 3. Speak about stereotyping.	**Independent Task:** Write about a group that you have stereotyped or that you know has been stereotyped based on language.	**Identifying and Using Main Ideas and Details:** Learn how to use main ideas and details to understand or express important points.

Speaking	Writing	Skill Focus
Independent Task: Give your opinion about the controversial tourist attraction.	**Integrated Task:** 1. Read about vacationing in Antarctica. 2. Listen to a lecture against tourism in Antarctica. 3. Write a summary of the lecture; explain how it contradicts ideas in the reading.	**Paraphrasing:** Learn how to restate ideas and information without changing the original meaning.
Integrated Task: 1. Read about humor research. 2. Listen to a joke told on a call-in radio program. 3. Explain the joke using theories from the reading.	**Independent Task:** Write about a TV show or movie that you thought was funny.	**Summarizing:** Learn how to understand summaries and to report information, leaving out less important details.
Independent Task: Give your opinion about dress codes or uniform policies in schools.	**Integrated Task:** 1. Read an argument against cosmetic surgery. 2. Listen to an excerpt about cosmetic improvements and surgery throughout history. 3. Write about the risks and benefits of cosmetic surgery.	**Comparing and Contrasting:** Learn how to recognize and discuss similarities and differences.
Integrated Task: 1. Read an argument against the death penalty. 2. Listen to an argument supporting execution. 3. Speak about the arguments for and against the death penalty.	**Independent Task:** Write about punishments that you think are appropriate for serious crimes.	**Using Detailed Examples:** Learn how to use and recognize examples that support and illustrate general statements.
Independent Task: With a partner, compare and contrast your views on marriage.	**Integrated Task:** 1. Read about polygamy. 2. Listen to an excerpt about marriage in the Mormon religion. 3. Write a summary of the reading; use supporting examples from the listening.	**Identifying and Using Cohesive Devices:** Learn how to recognize and use terms that connect ideas.

Introduction to NorthStar

Building Skills for the TOEFL iBT
Teacher's Manual

In cooperation with ETS®

Instructional Test Preparation

The TOEFL has changed, so preparation for it must change, too. Pearson Longman and ETS have combined their expertise in language learning and test development to create *NorthStar: Building Skills for the TOEFL iBT*. This three-level series takes a new approach—an instructional approach —to test preparation. The series links learning and assessment with a skill-building curriculum that incorporates authentic test material from the writers of the TOEFL iBT.

The TOEFL iBT requires students to show their ability to use English in a variety of campus and academic situations. These include listening to lectures on unfamiliar topics, orally paraphrasing and integrating information that they have just read and listened to, and writing a well-organized written response with detailed examples, correct grammar, and varied vocabulary. The speaking and writing tasks require clear and confident expression. With these books, students move progressively, sharpening language skills and test-taking abilities.

The three *Building Skills* texts are intended as stepping stones from classroom instruction in English to TOEFL and academic readiness. In language instruction, students will benefit most from an integrated skills, content-based curriculum, with a focus on critical thinking. In instructional test preparation with these books, students will encounter the same content-rich material, tasks, and question types that appear on the test. Using these books in the classroom will improve students' communicative skills, keep their interest, and sharpen awareness of their skills.

The TOEFL iBT

The new TOEFL iBT is an Internet-based test (iBT) that consists of four sections: Listening, Reading, Speaking, and Writing. The *NorthStar: Building Skills* texts feature many of the question types used on the TOEFL iBT. The books concentrate especially on preparing students for the newest and most difficult questions: the integrated tasks. These questions require test takers to

- read, listen, then speak in response to a question.
- listen, then speak in response to a question.
- read, listen, then write in response to a question.

The new integrated tasks that combine more than one skill are designed to reflect how we really use language. By preparing for the new TOEFL test, students will be building the skills they need to use language in an academic setting and communicate with confidence.

The second part of each *NorthStar: Building Skills for the TOEFL iBT* student book provides authentic practice and assessment materials developed by ETS. This material includes four listening lectures and conversations with questions, two reading passages with questions, two integrated writing tasks, and two integrated speaking tasks. Answers to all questions, as well as key points for the writing and speaking tasks, follow the practice section. Scoring Rubrics used by ETS-trained TOEFL iBT raters are also included. Students and instructors can review these rubrics to become familiar with the official guidelines used to assess student responses.

Language Instruction: With *NorthStar* or as Stand-alone Test Preparation

NorthStar: Building Skills for the TOEFL iBT Intermediate, High Intermediate, and Advanced can be used effectively with the corresponding *NorthStar* academic English series or on their own.

Students using *Building Skills* with the *NorthStar* series will find the same intellectually challenging themes. Listening and reading passages are drawn from *NorthStar* but exploited for different purposes. Though learners revisit some of the vocabulary, grammar, skills, and ideas in each *NorthStar* unit, all tasks and questions are new and tailored to reflect those of the TOEFL iBT. Thus, with the *Building Skills* books, students hone academic skills with familiar content.

Students using *Building Skills* as stand-alone test preparation will find ten thematic units in each book presenting contemporary and sophisticated listening and reading material. They will learn both new content and new vocabulary as they practice key language skills in tasks and questions that reflect those of the TOEFL iBT.

Whether using the *Building Skills* books alone or with *NorthStar,* learners of English engage with high-interest listening and reading material that reinforces language skills. At the same time, this rich material teaches, both implicitly and explicitly, ten key academic skills for TOEFL success. The books pay particular attention to the newest and most challenging TOEFL iBT tasks, helping students gain the confidence and speed they need to complete these tasks at high-scoring levels:

- listening for pragmatic understanding, or inference (attitude, degree of certainty, purpose, or motivation) in both campus conversations and academic listenings
- integrated tasks in speaking and writing
- independent tasks (expressing opinions) in speaking and writing

Unit Format in the Student Book

The first part of each book in the *Building Skills* series has ten units that are organized, like the TOEFL iBT, into Listening, Reading, Speaking, and Writing sections. Each unit also includes a Skill Focus section that explores one of the ten key academic language skills.

1 Listening

CAMPUS CONVERSATION

PRE-LISTENING VOCABULARY

To aid listening comprehension, students work with essential vocabulary and expressions in sentence-level contexts. They practice using context clues to identify meaning as well as practice pronunciation of new vocabulary.

CULTURE NOTE

Students read and react to important issues and practices in colleges and universities. The culture note can be a springboard for class discussion about students' experiences. It is important to address this note in class because most or all of the information will be very new to many students.

FIRST LISTENING

Students listen for main ideas and pragmatic understanding in a campus-related conversation and take notes on a separate piece of paper. (They should leave extra space in their notes so they can add more information.) Then students should compare answers. They answer the First Listening questions based on their notes.

SECOND LISTENING

Students listen again for main ideas, as well as for details, specific information, and additional pragmatic understanding. They should add information to the notes they took during the First Listening. They answer the questions based on their notes. For most inference questions, students listen again to an excerpt from the conversation before answering the question. Students are encouraged to compare and discuss their answers.

ACADEMIC LISTENING

FIRST LISTENING

Students listen for main ideas and pragmatic understanding in an academic lecture or interview, and take notes on a separate piece of paper. (They should leave extra space in their notes so they can add more information after each step.) Then students should compare answers. They answer the First Listening questions based on their notes.

SECOND LISTENING

Students listen again for main ideas, as well as for details, specific information, and pragmatic understanding. They should add information to the notes they took during the First Listening. For most inference questions, students listen again to an excerpt from the passage before answering the question. Students are encouraged to compare and discuss their answers.

ANALYSIS

The purpose of the analysis section is to familiarize students with TOEFL iBT question types. Students analyze their responses in order to identify skills requiring additional practice. In even-numbered units, students individually analyze and label each question from the Academic Listening section according to three categories: Basic Comprehension, Organization, and Inference. In odd-numbered units, students individually analyze and label each question from the Reading section according to four categories: Basic Comprehension, Organization, Inference, and Vocabulary and Reference. They compare their answers in pairs, check answers against the Answer Key, and discuss how to improve related skills.

2 Reading

PRE-READING

Before reading, students practice a pre-reading skill to help them comprehend the passage that follows. In many cases, this activity practices the Skill Focus of the unit.

READING

Students read the passage and work individually to answer questions focusing on main idea, details, paraphrasing, organizational pattern (rhetorical structure), inference, vocabulary, reference, summary, and categorization. Students are encouraged to compare and discuss their answers.

3 Speaking/Writing

INTEGRATED TASK: READ, LISTEN, SPEAK/WRITE

The Integrated Task is both receptive and productive. The purpose of this task is to have students synthesize information from a reading and a listening source (receptive) in order to provide an oral or written sample of their English (productive).

READING

Students read a short excerpt related to the theme of the unit. The excerpt is generally in textbook or essay style. Students take brief notes on main ideas and details to prepare for the productive task.

LISTENING

Students listen to an excerpt related to the theme of the unit. The excerpt is generally a segment of a professor's lecture, a dialogue, or an interview. The content of the listening excerpt often casts doubt on or presents a different perspective on the information in the reading. Or, it may exemplify or expand on that information. Students take notes on main ideas and details as they listen.

SPEAKING/WRITING

For speaking tasks, students prepare a short one-minute oral presentation in response to a topic question. Alternatively, they may prepare an interactive mini-debate, short role play or interview. For writing tasks, students prepare a paragraph-level response to the question within a 20-minute time frame. Students work together to prepare their individual responses to the topic question. Students can self-evaluate or be evaluated by their peers or teacher using the Speaking or Writing Evaluation Forms included at the back of the student books. In addition, teachers can utilize the TOEFL iBT Speaking Task or Writing Task Scoring Rubrics included in both the student books and Teacher's Manuals. (See pages B-7–B-10, B-16, B-30–B-33, B-45, B-56–B-61 of this Teacher's Manual for more information on *TOEFL iBT Scoring Rubrics.*)

4 Speaking/Writing

INDEPENDENT TASK

The purpose of the Independent Task is to give students an opportunity to produce an organized one-minute oral response or 20-minute written response related to the theme of the unit. The topic question asks students to express their opinions and give support using examples from their own life experience or the experiences of others. To prepare for this activity, groups or pairs of students follow a series of steps to brainstorm, gather ideas, and narrow the focus of their responses. As with the Integrated Tasks, students can self-evaluate or be evaluated by their peers or teacher using the techniques described above.

5 Skill Focus

Each unit focuses on one of ten essential skills for success on the TOEFL (see list on page xiv).

EXAMINATION

In the first phase of the Skill Focus section, Examination, students revisit items and tasks from the unit in order to focus on one skill area.

TIPS

The Skill Focus section continues with a series of tips that gives students more information about the skill and provides information that students can apply to related items on the TOEFL iBT. The teacher may want to use the tips as a springboard for class discussion. Do the students already use the skill? How might they develop the skill further as they prepare for the TOEFL iBT?

PRACTICE

Finally, students are given an opportunity to practice using the skill in a new activity related to the theme of the unit. They complete exercises that range from text analysis to editing to production tasks. These exercises enable students to assess their strengths and weaknesses in using the skill and applying it to answer TOEFL iBT–style items and tasks.

The 10 Essential TOEFL iBT Skills

To succeed on the TOEFL iBT, test takers must demonstrate what they can *do* with English, not simply what they *know about* English. To get a high score, it is not effective to memorize grammatical rules and definitions or master guessing strategies. Instead, students need to learn English well, and recognize and master ten key academic language skills. These are sophisticated language skills that require high levels of performance in listening/speaking, reading/writing, vocabulary, and grammar. The Skill Focus section in each unit of the *Building Skills* texts highlights and practices one key skill. Additionally, tasks throughout the unit offer both implicit and explicit practice of the focus skill. All three levels of *Building Skills* offer students the opportunity to solidify their awareness and mastery of these ten crucial skills.

1. SKIMMING AND SCANNING

Skimming is the ability to read a passage quickly to understand the gist, the general meaning, or the main idea. Scanning is the ability to read a passage quickly to find specific information, such as facts, names, and dates. Both skills are essential for reading efficiently for main ideas, details, inferences, and structure.

2. IDENTIFYING AND USING MAIN IDEAS AND DETAILS

The ability to identify main ideas and details shows understanding of a writer's or speaker's most important point as well as the way that point is supported. In writing, it is necessary to present clear main ideas as thesis statements and topic sentences and to support them with appropriate details. In speech, it is also important to present clear main ideas with supporting details so that listeners can follow a line of thinking easily.

3. MAKING INFERENCES

Making inferences is the ability to move beyond the literal meaning of a text to make guesses, predictions, or conclusions about information that is not stated directly. Students also "read between the lines" to infer a writer's intended meaning by using context clues. Students also "listen between the lines" to infer a speaker's intended meaning, attitude, and feelings by focusing on intonation, stress patterns, or tone of voice.

4. IDENTIFYING AND USING RHETORICAL STRUCTURE

Identifying rhetorical structure is the ability to recognize how a passage is organized and to understand the relationships among facts and ideas in different parts of the passage. It is also the ability to determine how and why speakers and writers use particular organizational structures to make their points and to identify connections—both implicit and explicit—among the parts of a passage. In writing and speech, it is important to know how to use rhetorical structure to present information in an organized form that distinguishes between major and minor points, to present steps in a process or narration, and to separate categories of information.

5. USING CONTEXT CLUES

Using context clues means using surrounding information in a written or spoken passage to figure out unknown words or phrases, to understand the relationship of details within the passage, and to make inferences.

6. PARAPHRASING

Identifying a paraphrase is the ability to recognize phrases or sentences that have the same meaning as other phrases or sentences, both when the vocabulary and grammatical structures are similar and when they are different. Using paraphrasing in writing and speech means restating ideas from another source in one's own words (different vocabulary and grammar) without changing the essential meaning of the original source.

7. SUMMARIZING

Summarizing is the ability to identify and extract the main ideas and details from a written or spoken passage, leaving out less important details, and then to reproduce this information in coherent writing or speech.

8. USING DETAILED EXAMPLES

Using detailed examples in writing or in speech shows the ability to illustrate an idea and to support general statements with concrete information.

9. COMPARING AND CONTRASTING

Identifying compare and contrast structures shows knowledge of expressions that point out likenesses and differences, the ability to analyze information in terms of similarities and differences, and the ability to distinguish two points of view. In writing and speech, comparing and contrasting are the abilities to express ideas by categorizing them into different parts, showing how they are similar or different, and how one casts doubt on another.

10. IDENTIFYING AND USING COHESIVE DEVICES

Identifying cohesive devices gives the reader or listener the ability to understand words and phrases that connect parts of a written or spoken text and signal the type of organization used (steps in a process, compare and contrast, cause and effect, and so on). In writing and speech, using cohesive devices, such as signal words *(therefore, similarly,* and *so)* and transitional phrases *(although this may be true, as an illustration,* and *for the same reason),* demonstrates the ability to introduce new information or ideas and to connect ideas in order to help the reader or listener understand the sequencing of ideas.

Note Taking for Comprehension and Planning

Throughout the TOEFL iBT, note taking is recommended to aid comprehension and memory, as well as to plan for speaking and writing tasks. The *Building Skills* texts provide ample practice in structured and semi-structured note-taking tasks in each unit at every level. For comprehension, students practice organizing, fleshing out, and using their notes to answer items. They learn to improve their notes by comparing them with those of peers, going back to the text or listening again to the audio material, and finally checking answers in the Answer Key. For planning, learners build on these note-taking skills by using the notes to organize their responses to speaking and writing items. The Teacher's Manuals provide additional suggestions for discussing note-taking styles (for example, outlines and charts) and tips (for example, taking notes on lectures, using abbreviations, and for phasing in independent or "blank-page" note taking).

Approach to Giving Feedback

The new Speaking section of the TOEFL iBT has six separate tasks: two on familiar topics, two on campus topics, and two on academic topics. In addition to topic development, the responses are scored on delivery (fluency and pronunciation) and language use (grammar, vocabulary).

The new Writing section of the TOEFL iBT has two separate tasks: (1) the familiar Independent Task, a written opinion in response to a general question, and (2) the new Integrated Task, a synthesis task requiring students to identify and paraphrase three main points in the reading and the three counterarguments in the listening. Both tasks are scored on organization and appropriate use of grammar and vocabulary. In addition, the response to the Independent Task is evaluated for development, while the response to the Integrated Task is evaluated for the completeness and accuracy of the content.

With *Building Skills,* students have many opportunities to practice these speaking and writing tasks. In the classroom setting, teachers are encouraged to help students internalize the TOEFL iBT time limits and scoring standards, monitor themselves, and begin to perceive their improvement. In optional peer feedback tasks, students use the Speaking and Writing Evaluation Forms at the back of the Student Books to assess one another's responses and to develop awareness of their own strengths and weaknesses.

The Teacher's Manuals give suggestions for using both the Evaluation Forms and the TOEFL iBT Scoring Rubrics to give feedback on the Integrated and Independent Speaking and Writing tasks. They also provide detailed information on how to score tasks, as well as model responses at different score levels for reference.

Enhancing Classroom Interaction with the Texts

Since the TOEFL iBT emphasizes communication, it is fitting that preparation for the test have the same emphasis. In instructional test preparation, students develop communicative skills through interaction in a classroom setting. Not only do they practice skills, but they also help, encourage, and learn to critique one another. To do well on the test, students need to comprehend and recognize text features as well as produce them in speaking and writing. Through constant interaction with classmates, they build the awareness, skill, and confidence to perform.

Overview of the Teacher's Manuals

The *NorthStar: Building Skills for the TOEFL iBT* Teacher's Manuals feature:

SCOPE AND SEQUENCE

PART ONE: UNIT-BY-UNIT TEACHING SUGGESTIONS

Specific suggestions for teaching each unit, including

- Unit-by-unit overview
- Unit-by-unit description of the Focus, Setup, and Expansion (including homework) activities for each section
- Suggested teaching times
- Suggestions for discussing note-taking styles and strategies
- Suggestions for teaching reporting verbs that are useful for the TOEFL iBT

PART TWO: ETS SCORING GUIDE FOR TOEFL iBT INSTRUCTORS

Extensive guidance in assessing students' written and spoken responses, including

- Description from ETS of Independent and Integrated Writing and Speaking tasks and scoring guidelines
- Authentic TOEFL iBT Scoring Rubrics with evaluation criteria
- Examples of authentic student responses graded at each score level with annotations
- Practice sets that allow teachers to practice applying the scoring criteria to authentic student responses

APPENDICES

A: Signal Words and Phrases
B: Transition Words and Phrases

PART ONE

Unit-by-Unit
Teaching Suggestions

Advertising

| LISTENING |

Campus Conversation   A student talks to a professor about false advertising.

Academic Listening   Radio Ads: *Advertising on the Air*

| READING |

Essay   *Changing World Markets*

| SPEAKING |

Integrated Task: Use examples from the reading and listening
Read, Listen, Speak   excerpts to explain emotional appeals in advertising.

| WRITING |

Independent Task   Write about a product you enjoy and explain how
to advertise it.

| SKILL FOCUS |

Skimming and Scanning   Skimming is reading quickly to understand the
general meaning, the gist. Scanning is reading
quickly to find specific information, such as names
and dates.

| TOEFL® iBT TARGET SKILLS |

- Identify and express main ideas
- Identify and express details
- Make inferences
- Organize information
- Make predictions
- Take notes and complete an outline
- Summarize and compare information

 For extra practice of
TOEFL iBT skills, go to
pages 208–226 of the
Student Book.

1 Listening

CAMPUS CONVERSATION

PRE-LISTENING VOCABULARY
Suggested Time: 15 minutes

Focus
To acquaint students with useful vocabulary, including campus vocabulary; to aid comprehension of the conversation; to give practice inferring word meaning from context

Setup
Look at the directions as a class. Be sure each student has a partner to work with. Ask students to read each sentence with their partner and to discuss the meaning of the boldfaced words and phrases without looking at the choices below. Circulate around the room to check students' pronunciation and correct when appropriate. Encourage students to guess the meaning, but make informed guesses based on the context of the sentences. Then have students complete the exercise independently. Finally, they should confirm their answers with their partners. Students can check with other pairs or the teacher if there is disagreement.

Expansion
(1) If class time is limited, you may want to assign the exercise as homework and use class time to check answers and correct pronunciation. (2) To help students memorize vocabulary, have them work in pairs to quiz each other on the definitions. (3) For homework, ask students to write one original sentence for each vocabulary item. Collect these sentences from the students in the next class. Then make a vocabulary study sheet for the students using 2 to 3 of the most exemplary sentences for each vocabulary item.

CULTURE NOTE
Suggested Time: 5 minutes

Focus
To inform students about important aspects of life at colleges and universities

Setup
Ask a student to read the Culture Note aloud. Then ask the class to brainstorm specific topics a student might ask a professor during office hours.

Expansion
(1) Have students share any stories they might have about professors' office hours. (2) Have students write, in class or as homework, about an experience they or someone they know might have had about the culture topic. (3) Have

students do Internet research. Ask them to go to a college website and try to find general information about professors' office hours or about a specific professors' office hours. Have them share their information in class.

FIRST LISTENING
Suggested Time: 15 minutes

Focus

To help students listen for the main ideas in a campus-based conversation

Setup

Have students read the questions before listening. Play the conversation only once. Have students take notes related to the questions as they listen. Then have students work in pairs to share notes and answer the questions.

Expansion

(1) For this first unit, you may want to discuss the role of note taking and note-taking skills, such as using symbols and abbreviations, not writing in complete sentences, and organizing information on the page. (2) You may want students to wait to compare their notes about the main ideas until after they have listened a second time (during Second Listening). Then students may discuss what information helped them find *main ideas* and what information helped them find *details*.

SECOND LISTENING
Suggested Time: 25 minutes

Focus

To have students listen again, this time for details, specific information, and additional pragmatic understanding

Setup

Have students read all of the questions on their own. Stress that they should not take time to answer the questions. The purpose in reading the questions is to familiarize themselves with the questions to focus their listening. Have students review their First Listening notes to see which ideas and details they have already included. Play the conversation again. Have students add to their First Listening notes. Then have students answer the Second Listening items. Encourage them to use their notes. Finally, have students compare answers with a classmate. If they have different answers, replay the conversation rather than give the answer.

Expansion

(1) You may want to model note taking for the students by playing the conversation a third time and taking notes on the board or on an overhead. Students can then compare their notes to yours, and you can discuss the differences. (2) You may want to have students use their notes and their Second Listening answers to role-play the conversation in pairs. Focus on the entire conversation or one particular part. Review with students pronunciation, stress and intonation patterns. Listen to individual pairs and give feedback. Use the Speaking Evaluation Form on page 180 of the student book.

ACADEMIC LISTENING

FIRST LISTENING
Suggested Time: 15 minutes

Focus
To help students listen for the main ideas in two radio ads; to practice note taking

Setup
Read the directions as a class. Ask students to look at the chart and read the information already given. Ask them to predict what kind of products they will hear about in the ads. Play the radio ads only once. Have students take notes to complete the information in the chart as they listen. Then, in pairs, have students compare their charts.

Expansion
You may want students to wait to compare their charts until after they have finished the Second Listening. Students may discuss which information they consider is essential to include in the chart. Then students may discuss which notes they added when they listened to the radio ads a second time.

SECOND LISTENING
Suggested Time: 30 minutes

Focus
To have students listen again, this time for details, specific information, and pragmatic understanding

Setup
Have students read all of the questions on their own. Stress that they should not take time to answer the questions. The purpose in reading the questions is to familiarize themselves with the questions to focus their listening. Have students review their First Listening notes to see which ideas and details they have already included. Play the radio ads again. Have students add details to their charts. Then have students answer the Second Listening items. Encourage them to use their notes. Finally, have students compare answers with a classmate. If they have different answers, replay the ads rather than give the answer.

Expansion
(1) Ask students to work in small groups and discuss a memorable TV commercial (or print ad) that the members of their group like. Have the groups report back to the class. In doing so they should (a) say what the product or service is, (b) describe the ad, and (c) say why it is memorable, including emotional appeal, if appropriate. Have classmates evaluate each other, using the Speaking Evaluation form on page 180 of the student book. (2) This activity can also be assigned as homework in which students write about a memorable ad.

2 Reading

PRE-READING
Suggested Time: 5 minutes

Focus
To preview the reading, make predictions about the content, and practice skimming and scanning skills

Setup
Read the directions as a class. Have students work independently to skim the first and last sentences of each paragraph and underline them. Then have students work in pairs to brainstorm ideas and predict the content of the reading.

Expansion
(1) Have pairs compare their ideas with another pair and have them combine their notes. Then have one student in each group report to the class on his/her group's ideas. (2) Explain to students that skimming, a type of quick reading, is an important skill that will help them on the TOEFL iBT, and they will practice it again later in the unit. Have them discuss why they think skimming and scanning are important.

READING
Suggested Time: 45 minutes

Focus
To give practice reading for main ideas, details and inference, understanding vocabulary in context, and recognizing rhetorical style; to learn about advertising strategies in the world market

Setup
Have students preview the questions before they read the passage. This will help them focus their attention. Then give them 15 to 20 minutes to read and answer the questions. Have students compare their answers with a partner. If disagreements about answers arise, encourage students to review the reading text.

Expansion
(1) Encourage students to take notes as they read or to highlight important information in the margins. (2) If class time is limited, you may want to assign the reading and questions as homework and use the class time to compare and discuss answers. (3) For Unit 1, explain the question types; i.e., main idea, detail, vocabulary, inference, etc. See the Analysis section in the Answer Key for reference. Explain that these are the types of questions students will see on the TOEFL iBT.

ANALYSIS
Suggested Time: 15 minutes

Focus
To familiarize students with TOEFL iBT question types; to teach students to analyze their responses in order to identify skills requiring additional practice

Setup
Review with students the four types of reading questions fully, and invite students to ask questions about them. You may want to describe the features of each type, using individual question items as examples. Have students identify the question types on their own and compare their answers in pairs or small groups.

Expansion
(1) For Unit 1, you may want to do the Analysis section with the class—or at least one item of each kind. (2) You may also want to tally the results and see which type of questions students are having trouble with. For problem types, you may want to refer students to the related Skill Focus section at the end of each unit for more information and practice. After the students have categorized the items on their own, discuss the items as a group.

3 Speaking

INTEGRATED TASK: READ, LISTEN, SPEAK

Focus
To synthesize information from a short reading and listening and then speak a response

Setup
Review the sequence of activities that students will practice in the Integrated Skill section. These activities reflect the Integrated speaking and writing sections of the TOEFL iBT. Students will need to integrate their skills: They will read a short text and listen to an excerpt on a related topic and then, in this unit, speak about emotional appeals in ads using examples from both the reading and the listening passages. Explain that in every other unit, students will do a writing task in response to the two excerpts.

Expansion
You may want to preview the content of the reading and listening sections by telling students that the reading describes an advertising campaign that worked well in Australia but failed in the United States. The listening passage describes various advertising techniques.

READING
Suggested Time: 30 minutes

Focus
To give students practice in summarizing a short text

Setup
Have students read the passage on their own and then work with a partner to complete the task.

Expansion
(1) You may tell students to take notes on a separate piece of paper as they read and then combine their notes with a partner's. These notes can then be shared with the class; however, eventually students will need to be able to complete these tasks efficiently on their own. (2) If class time is limited, assign the reading and note taking as homework.

LISTENING
Suggested Time: 30 minutes

Focus
To help students identify the main idea and details in a short listening passage; to complete an outline

Setup
Before students listen, have them look at the outline and read the main idea sentence aloud. Then have them take notes to fill in the outline as they listen.

Expansion
(1) You may want to discuss the role of note taking in this activity. Students will need these notes to prepare for the speaking task. Remind students about note-taking strategies such as using abbreviations and symbols. (2) You may want students to compare their notes in pairs or small groups. If disagreements about answers arise, play the excerpt again.

SPEAKING
Suggested Time: 20 minutes

Focus
To have students synthesize information from a reading text and a lecture and use the ideas in a spoken response

Setup
(1) Ask students to read the speaking topic. Have students work in pairs and have them read their notes from the reading and listening tasks. Then have them complete the outlines. (2) Before students continue with Step 2, introduce and explain the Speaking Evaluation Form on page 180 of the student book. (3) Have each partner give a one-minute oral response. Stress that students should use ideas from the reading and listening passages, not their own ideas. (4) Have students change partners and repeat the activity. Students may use the Speaking Evaluation Form to evaluate one or both of their partners.

Expansion

(1) After students have completed Step 3, ask for volunteers to present their response to the class. Give students individual feedback using the criteria on the Speaking Evaluation Form on page 180 and the TOEFL iBT Integrated Speaking Task Scoring Rubric on page 235 in the student book and on page B-16 in this manual. (2) On the TOEFL iBT, students will need to report the ideas of others. Below are some useful expressions students can use.

Expressions for reporting facts or ideas

EXPRESSIONS	EXAMPLES
say that	The professor **said that** the assignment is (was) due next week.
tell (someone) that	The professor **told _the class_ that** the assignment is (was) due next week.
point out that	The professor **pointed out that** the assignment is (was) due next week.

Emphasize with your students the difference between *say* and *tell*. They are similar in meaning; however, *tell* requires an indirect object (someone).

Expressions for giving an opinion

EXPRESSIONS	EXAMPLES
believe that	The professor **believed that** the student deserved an A+ instead of just an A.
think that	The professor **thought that** two weeks was enough time for the students to finish the project.
recommend that	The professor **recommended that** the students begin the term paper as soon as possible.

Note that *recommend that* belongs to a class of expressions that is followed by a subject plus the base form of the verb.

When teaching these expressions, ask students to retain the word *that*, even though it is technically optional. Tell your students that *that* is a reminder to them that a subject and a verb will come next.

Also, as an advanced or native speaker of English yourself, you know the rules for reported speech: the verb in the *that* clause "moves back" one tense. However, at this level and with these basic expressions, do not worry about teaching this point. If you force this rule too much, the English can sound unnatural. Furthermore, there are several exceptions to the rule (such as *recommend that*). When your students have a stronger sense of English, they will be able to integrate this rule into their production of English.

4 Writing

INDEPENDENT TASK

Suggested Time: 45 minutes

Focus

To give students an opportunity to produce an organized written response related to the theme of the unit using information from the unit and their own experiences

Setup

(1) Ask students to read the writing topic. Have students begin to work on their own and then work in a group to prepare for the writing task. Encourage students to use the discussion as an opportunity for brainstorming and to take notes during the conversation. (2) Before students write, introduce and explain the Writing Evaluation Form on page 179 of the student book. (3) Allow students to write for 20 minutes, and then remind them to use the last five minutes for proofreading and editing. The students can evaluate each other's writing using the Writing Evaluation Form. (4) Give students feedback using the criteria on the TOEFL iBT Independent Writing Task Scoring Rubric on page 234 of the student book and page B-33 in this manual.

Expansion

If time does not allow students to complete Step 2 in class, ask them to write at home, but to try to keep to the time limit.

5 Skill Focus

EXAMINATION

Suggested Time: 15 minutes

Focus

To have students examine items and tasks from the unit that focus on one essential skill assessed on the TOEFL; to reinforce a key skill that students have practiced in the unit

Setup

(1) Talk to students about the time involved in reading a text. Remind them that, when taking the TOEFL, they need to be conscious of how much time they spend on reading. Learning to skim and scan a text will enable them to read and answer questions more efficiently.

(2) Ask students to complete the Examination section. As a class, discuss their answers to the three questions on the bottom of page 13.

Expansion
You may have students work in pairs to complete the examination section.

TIPS
Suggested Time: 10 minutes

Focus
To give students more information about the focus skill; to provide information that students can apply to related items on the TOEFL iBT

Setup
(1) Remind students that different skills are required for different types of reading. Reading for pleasure does not require a person to think about the efficient use of time. When reading a passage on the TOEFL, using one's time wisely is important. (2) Have students read the Tips section. Then explain each tip and the example item(s) to which it refers.

Expansion
Give the class a short text. Use a short reading from a class textbook or level-appropriate newspaper or magazine. Give them some questions, perhaps two that require skimming and two that require scanning. Give the class just a few minutes to answer the questions. Afterwards, discuss strategies the students used to find the answers.

PRACTICE
Suggested Time: 30 minutes

Focus
To have students apply the knowledge from the Skill Focus section; to help students improve their skimming and scanning skills

Setup
Review the tips for skimming and scanning with the class. Ask the students if they have any questions. Then ask them to read the directions on page 15 and complete the practice activities.

Expansion
Give students one or more short texts to read. For each text, give a few questions to answer by skimming or scanning.

Extreme Sports

| LISTENING |

Campus Conversation
A student talks to a professor about her parents' expectations concerning her plan of study.

Academic Listening
Lecture: *Sensation Seekers*

| READING |

Newspaper Article
High School Star Hospitalized for Eating Disorder

| WRITING |

**Integrated Task:
Read, Listen, Write**
Relate the different meanings of the word *obsession* to the experience of Tony Hawk, the skateboarder.

| SPEAKING |

Independent Task
Describe a time in your life when you did something obsessively.

| SKILL FOCUS |

Making Inferences
Inferences are guesses, predictions, or conclusions about information that is not stated directly.

| TOEFL® iBT TARGET SKILLS |

- Identify and express main ideas
- Identify and express details
- Take notes and complete an outline
- Relate an abstract idea to concrete information
- Infer a speaker's or writer's intention or purpose

 For extra practice of TOEFL iBT skills, go to pages 208–226 of the Student Book.

1 Listening

CAMPUS CONVERSATION

PRE-LISTENING VOCABULARY
Suggested Time: 15 minutes

Focus
To acquaint students with useful vocabulary, including campus vocabulary; to aid comprehension of the conversation; to give practice inferring word meaning from context

Setup
Look at the directions as a class. Be sure each student has a partner to work with. Ask students to read each sentence with their partners and to discuss the meaning of the boldfaced words and phrases without looking at the choices below. Circulate around the room to check students' pronunciation and correct when appropriate. Encourage students to guess the meaning but make informed guesses based on the context of the sentences. Then have students complete the exercise independently. Finally, they should confirm their answers with their partners. Students can check with other pairs or the teacher if there is disagreement.

Expansion
(1) If class time is limited, you may want to assign the exercise as homework and use class time to check answers and correct pronunciation. (2) To help students memorize vocabulary, have them work in pairs to quiz each other on the definitions. (3) To introduce the skill focus in this unit—making inferences—you may want to point out that when doing the vocabulary exercise, students should use the surrounding context to help them infer, or guess, the meaning of the target words. (4) For homework, ask students to write one original sentence for each vocabulary item. Collect these sentences from the students in the next class. Then make a vocabulary study sheet for the students using 2 to 3 of the most exemplary sentences for each vocabulary item.

CULTURE NOTE
Suggested Time: 5 minutes

Focus
To inform students about important aspects of life at colleges and universities

Setup
Students may not feel comfortable talking in class about grading. If they are not comfortable talking about grading, simply ask them to read the culture note. If they are, ask them to talk about a grade they received that they had to work hard to earn. Then ask students to read the Culture Note about grading.

Expansion

(1) If students are comfortable discussing grading, have them share any interesting experiences they may have had concerning their grades. (2) Have students interview a professor about the grading policy in his/her class. Students may share any information they learned in the next class.

FIRST LISTENING
Suggested Time: 15 minutes

Focus

To help students listen for the main ideas in a campus-based conversation

Setup

Have students read the questions before listening. Play the conversation only once. Have students take notes related to the questions as they listen. Then have students work in pairs to share notes and answer the questions.

Expansion

(1) Review note-taking conventions that you discussed in Unit 1. (2) Have students compare the notes they have taken here to the notes they took in Unit 1. Has their note-taking skill improved? Ask what they can do to further develop their skills.

SECOND LISTENING
Suggested Time: 25 minutes

Focus

To have students listen again, this time for details, specific information, and additional pragmatic understanding

Setup

Have students read the Second Listening questions and review their First Listening notes to see which ideas and details they have already included. Play the conversation again. Have students add to their First Listening notes. Then have students answer the Second Listening items. Encourage them to use their notes. Finally, have students compare answers with a classmate.

Expansion

(1) If pairs of students disagree on their answers, have them listen to the passage again. Then review the answers as a class. (2) You may want to have students use their notes and their Second Listening answers to role-play the conversation in pairs. Focus on the entire conversation or one particular part. Review with students pronunciation, stress, and intonation patterns. Listen to individual pairs and give feedback. Use the Speaking Evaluation Form on page 180 of the student book.

ACADEMIC LISTENING

FIRST LISTENING
Suggested Time: 15 minutes

Focus
To help students listen for the main ideas in a short lecture

Setup
Read the directions as a class. Ask students to look at the chart and read the information already given. Ask them to predict what they will hear about in the lecture. Play the lecture only once. Have students take notes to complete the information in the chart as they listen. Then, in pairs, have students compare their charts.

Expansion
You may want students to wait to compare their charts until after they have finished the Second Listening. Students may discuss which information they consider is essential to include in the chart. Then, students may discuss which notes they added when they listened to the lecture a second time.

SECOND LISTENING
Suggested Time: 30 minutes

Focus
To have students listen again, this time for details, specific information, and pragmatic understanding

Setup
Have students read all of the questions on their own. Stress that they should not take time to answer the questions. The purpose in reading the questions is to familiarize themselves with the questions to focus their listening. Have students review their First Listening notes to see which ideas and details they have already included. Play the lecture again. Have students add details to their charts. Then have students answer the Second Listening items. Encourage them to use their notes. Finally, have students compare answers with a classmate. If they have different answers, replay the lecture rather than give the answer.

Expansion
(1) Have students work in small groups and talk about *"sensation seekers"* they may know personally or may have read about. Ask, "What jobs do these people have? What kinds of things do they enjoy?" (2) Have students write a short paragraph in class or for homework giving their reaction to information in the lecture.

ANALYSIS
Suggested Time: 15 minutes

Focus
To familiarize students with TOEFL iBT question types; to teach students to analyze their responses in order to identify skills requiring additional practice

Setup
Explain the three types of listening questions fully, and invite students to ask questions about them. You may want to describe the features of each type, using individual question items as examples. Have students identify the question types on their own and compare their answers in pairs or small groups.

Expansion
(1) You may want to do the Analysis section with the class—or at least one item of each kind. (2) You may also want to tally the results and see which type of questions students are having trouble with. For problem types, you may want to refer students to the related Skill Focus section at the end of each unit for more information and practice. After the students have categorized the items on their own, discuss the items as a group.

2 Reading

PRE-READING
Suggested Time: 5 minutes

Focus
To preview the reading, make predictions about the content and practice skimming and scanning skills

Setup
Read the directions as a class. Have students work independently to skim the first sentence of each paragraph and underline it. Then have students work in pairs to brainstorm ideas and predict the content of the reading. Have them write the answers to the questions. They may use a separate piece of paper to write their answers.

Expansion
You may want to have students share their answers in small groups. Encourage some students to share their answers with the entire class and discuss the responses. To highlight the focus skill in this unit, have students discuss the strategies they used to answer the questions. Ask, "What clues (words or phrases) helped you find the answers to the questions?"

READING
Suggested Time: 45 minutes

Focus
To give practice reading for main ideas, details and inference, understanding vocabulary in context, and recognizing rhetorical style; to learn about an athlete who developed anorexia nervosa

Setup
Have students preview the questions before they read the passage. This will help them focus their attention. Then give them 15 to 20 minutes to read and answer the questions. Have students compare their answers with a partner. If disagreements about answers arise, encourage students to review the reading text.

Expansion
(1) Encourage students to take notes as they read or to highlight important information in the margins. (2) If class time is limited, you may want to assign the reading and questions as homework and use the class time to compare and discuss answers. (3) The section on analyzing reading questions appears in every other unit; however, you may want to have students analyze the question types in this unit as well.

3 Writing

INTEGRATED TASK: READ, LISTEN, WRITE

Focus
To synthesize information from a short reading and listening and then write a response

Setup
Review the sequence of activities that students will practice in the Integrated Skill section. These activities reflect the Integrated speaking and writing sections of the TOEFL iBT. Students will need to integrate their skills; they will read a short text and listen to an excerpt on a related topic and then, in this unit, write about obsession and how it relates to Tony Hawk, the professional skateboarder.

Expansion
You many want to preview the content of the reading and listening sections by telling students that the reading includes two different definitions of the word *obsession*. The listening passage is part of an interview with Tony Hawk, the professional skateboarder.

READING
Suggested Time: 30 minutes

Focus
To practice reading definitions and applying them to concepts in the unit

Setup
Have students read the definitions on their own and then work with a partner to complete the task.

Expansion
(1) After students read the definitions and before they answer the question, you may want to tell student pairs to make two lists of words—one that describes sensation seekers and one that describes people suffering from anorexia nervosa. Students may go back to the notes they took in the Academic Reading and Listening sections of the unit. Then they can more easily relate the definitions to the two groups of people. (2) You may tell students to take notes as they read and then combine their notes with a partner's. These notes can then be shared with the class; however, eventually students will need to be able to complete these tasks efficiently on their own. (3) If class time is limited, assign the reading and note taking as homework.

LISTENING
Suggested Time: 30 minutes

Focus
To help students identify the main idea and details in a short listening passage; to complete an outline

Setup
Before students listen, have them look at the outline and read the main idea sentence aloud. Then have them take notes to fill in the outline as they listen. They may use a separate piece of paper to take notes.

Expansion
(1) You may want to discuss the role of note taking in this activity. Students will need these notes to prepare for the speaking task. Remind students about note-taking strategies such as using abbreviations and symbols. (2) You may want students to compare their notes in pairs or small groups. If disagreements about answers arise, play the excerpt again.

WRITING
Suggested Time: 20 minutes

Focus
To have students synthesize information from a reading text and an interview and use the ideas in a written response.

Setup

(1) Ask students to read the writing topic. Have students work in pairs and have them read their notes from the reading and listening tasks. Then have them answer the questions. (2) Before students continue with Step 2, introduce and explain the Writing Evaluation Form on page 179 of the student book.

Expansion

(1) If time does not allow students to complete Step 2 in class, ask them to complete it as homework. Stress that they should take no more than 20 minutes to write, as this reflects the time constraints of the TOEFL iBT. (2) As suggested in Unit 1, you may want to include a brief activity on reported speech to help students incorporate textual information into their writing. Present common reporting verbs such as those in the list on page A-10. (3) After students have completed Step 2, ask students to submit their writing to you. Give students individual feedback using the criteria on the Writing Evaluation Form and the TOEFL iBT Integrated Writing Task Scoring Rubric on page 233 in the student book and on page B-45 in this manual.

4 Speaking

INDEPENDENT TASK

Suggested Time: 45 minutes

Focus

To have students respond to a question in an oral presentation, making recommendations and expressing and supporting their opinions with examples

Setup

Ask students to read the speaking topic. Go over the outline in Step 1 with the class to ensure that students understand what information to include. Step 2: Have students work with a partner to prepare for the speaking task. Step 3: Have students find new partners and take turns performing the speaking task. The students can evaluate each other's oral responses by using the Speaking Evaluation Form on page 180 of the student book.

Expansion

After students have completed Step 3, ask for volunteers to present their response to the class. To assess the presentation, use the Speaking Evaluation Form on page 180 or the TOEFL iBT Independent Speaking Task Scoring Rubric on page 236 in the student book or page B-10 of this manual.

5 Skill Focus

EXAMINATION
Suggested Time: 15 minutes

Focus
To have students examine items and tasks from the unit that focus on one essential skill assessed on the TOEFL iBT; to reinforce a key skill that students have practiced in the unit

Setup
(1) Talk to students about the meaning of the words *explicit* or *literal* and *inferred*. Inferring is the skill that allows a person to read or listen "between the lines" since not all ideas are explicitly stated. Meaning can be communicated with body language, tone of voice, and careful choice of words. (2) Ask students to complete the Examination section. As a class, discus their answers to the question on page 29.

Expansion
You may have students work in pairs to complete the Examination section.

TIPS
Suggested Time: 10 minutes

Focus
To give students more information about the focus skill; to provide information that students can apply to related items on the TOEFL iBT

Setup
Have students read the Tips section. Then explain each tip and the example item(s) to which it refers.

Expansion
If class time is limited, have students read this section at home and come prepared to the next class with questions and comments.

PRACTICE
Suggested Time: 30 minutes

Focus
To have students apply the knowledge from the Skill Focus section; to help students improve their skills to make inferences

Setup
Review the tips for making inferences with the class. Ask the students if they have any questions. Then ask them to read the directions on page 30 and complete the practice activities.

Expansion
Give students one or more short texts to read. For each text, give them a few questions to answer that require them to make inferences about the author's meaning, intention, or attitude.

Fraud

| LISTENING |

Campus Conversation A student talks to a financial aid advisor about scholarships.

Academic Listening Interviews: *Victims of Fraud*

| READING |

An Advertisement *The Organic Health Center*

| SPEAKING |

Integrated Task: Read, Listen, Speak Role play a situation that supports the points of view described in the listening and reading excerpts.

| WRITING |

Independent Task Describe an experience with fraud or dishonesty.

| SKILL FOCUS |

Using Context Clues Using context clues means using surrounding information in a written or spoken text to determine the meaning of unknown words or phrases.

| TOEFL® iBT TARGET SKILLS |

- Identify and express main ideas
- Identify and express details
- Make inferences
- Organize information in a chart
- Skim text to make predictions
- Outline information in a timeline

 For extra practice of TOEFL iBT skills, go to pages 208–226 of the Student Book.

1 Listening

CAMPUS CONVERSATION

PRE-LISTENING VOCABULARY
Suggested Time: 15 minutes

Focus
To acquaint students with useful vocabulary, including campus vocabulary; to aid comprehension of the conversation; to give practice inferring word meaning from context

Setup
Look at the directions as a class. Be sure each student has a partner to work with. Ask students to read each sentence with their partner and to discuss the meaning of the boldfaced words and phrases without looking at the choices below. Circulate around the room to check students' pronunciation and correct when appropriate. Encourage students to guess the meaning but make informed guesses based on the context of the sentences. Then have students complete the exercise independently. Finally, they should confirm their answers with their partners. Students can check with other pairs or the teacher if there is disagreement.

Expansion
(1) If class time is limited, you may want to assign the exercise as homework and use class time to check answers and correct pronunciation. (2) To help students memorize vocabulary, have them work in pairs to quiz each other on the definitions. (3) For homework, ask students to write one original sentence for each vocabulary item. Collect these sentences from the students in the next class. Then make a vocabulary study sheet for the students using 2 to 3 of the most exemplary sentences for each vocabulary item.

CULTURE NOTE
Suggested Time: 5 minutes

Focus
To inform students about important aspects of life at colleges and universities

Setup
Ask students to read the Culture Note. Ask them if they know of any organizations that offer college scholarships or any other means of funding higher education.

Expansion
Students could investigate sources of college scholarships and report back to the class.

FIRST LISTENING
Suggested Time: 15 minutes

Focus
To help students listen for the main ideas in a campus-based conversation

Setup
Have students read the questions before listening. Play the conversation only once. Have students take notes related to the questions as they listen. Then have students work in pairs to share notes and answer the questions.

Expansion
(1) Review the role of note taking and note-taking skills, such as using symbols and abbreviations, not writing in complete sentences, and organizing information on the page. (2) You may want students to wait to compare their notes about the main ideas until after they have listened a second time (during Second Listening). Then students may discuss what information helped them find *main ideas* and what information helped them find *details*.

SECOND LISTENING
Suggested Time: 25 minutes

Focus
To have students listen again, this time for details, specific information, and additional pragmatic understanding

Setup
Have students read all of the questions on their own. Stress that they should not take time to answer the questions. The purpose in reading the questions is to familiarize themselves with the questions to focus their listening. Have students review their First Listening notes to see which ideas and details they have already included. Play the conversation again. Have students add to their First Listening notes. Then have students answer the Second Listening items. Encourage them to use their notes. Finally, have students compare answers with a classmate. If they have different answers, replay the conversation rather than give the answer.

Expansion
For homework, ask students to research a scholarship search service on the Internet and report back to class.

ACADEMIC LISTENING

FIRST LISTENING
Suggested Time: 15 minutes

Focus
To help students listen for the main ideas in the interviews; to practice note taking

Setup

Read the directions as a class. Play the interviews only once. Have students take notes to complete the information in the chart as they listen. Then, in pairs, have students compare their charts.

Expansion

You may want students to wait to compare their charts until after they have finished the Second Listening. Students may discuss which information they consider is essential to include in the chart. Then students may discuss which notes they added when they listened to the interviews a second time.

SECOND LISTENING
Suggested Time: 30 minutes

Focus

To have students listen again, this time for details, specific information, and pragmatic understanding

Setup

Have students read all of the questions on their own. Stress that they should not take time to answer the questions. The purpose in reading the questions is to familiarize themselves with the questions to help their listening. Have students review their First Listening notes to see which ideas and details they have already included. Play the interviews again. Have students add details to their charts. Then have students answer the Second Listening items. Encourage them to use their notes. Finally, have students compare answers with a classmate. If they have different answers, replay the interviews rather than give the answer.

Expansion

(1) Each of the victims in the interviews had a different reason for believing Frank. Ask students to think back to the Campus Conversation and discuss which reason(s) might explain why students trust scholarship search services. (2) You may want to have students work in small groups and use their notes and their Second Listening answers to present role plays based on the interviews. Review with students pronunciation, stress, and intonation patterns. Listen to individual pairs and give feedback.

2. Reading

PRE-READING
Suggested Time: 5 minutes

Focus

To preview the reading, make predictions about the content, practice skimming and scanning skills, and guessing meaning from context

Setup

Read the instructions as a class. Students will find the meanings of these words by identifying context clues (the skill focus of this unit) in the text. After students have quickly read the text, ask them to compare their answers and report on what they have read.

Expansion

(1) Have students work in groups and discuss what strategies they used to find the meanings of the words. (2) Ask students to look the words up in a dictionary and compare the dictionary definitions to their definitions.

READING
Suggested Time: 45 minutes

Focus

To give practice reading for main ideas, details and inference, understanding vocabulary in context, and recognizing rhetorical style; to read about a clinic and its founder, who claims to offer a cure for cancer

Setup

Have students preview the questions before they read the passage. This will help them focus their attention. Then give them 15 to 20 minutes to read and answer the questions. Have students compare their answers with a partner. If disagreements about answers arise, encourage students to review the reading text.

Expansion

(1) Encourage students to take notes as they read or to highlight important information in the margins. (2) If class time is limited, you may want to assign the reading and questions as homework and use the class time to compare and discuss answers.

ANALYSIS
Suggested Time: 15 minutes

For a discussion of Reading Analysis, please refer to Unit 1, page A-8 in the Teacher's Manual.

3 Speaking

INTEGRATED TASK: READ, LISTEN, SPEAK

You many want to preview the content of the reading and listening sections by telling students that the reading is an excerpt from a magazine describing reasons why people might trust unproven medical treatments. The listening passage describes the story of Matt Bloomfield, an individual who discovered he had an incurable cancer.

READING
Suggested Time: 30 minutes

Focus
To help students identify the main ideas and important details in a reading

Setup
Have students read the passage on their own and then work with a partner to complete the task.

Expansion
(1) You may tell students to take notes on a separate piece of paper as they read and then combine their notes with a partner's. These notes can then be shared with the class; however, eventually students will need to be able to complete these tasks efficiently on their own. (2) If class time is limited, assign the reading and note taking as homework.

LISTENING
Suggested Time: 30 minutes

Focus
To help students identify the main idea and details in a short listening passage, to take notes and complete a timeline

Setup
Before students listen, have them look at the timeline and read the information that is filled in. Then have them take notes to fill in the timeline as they listen.

Expansion
You may want students to compare their notes in pairs or small groups. If disagreements about answers arise, play the excerpt again.

SPEAKING
Suggested Time: 20 minutes

Focus
To have students synthesize information from a reading text and a listening passage and use the ideas in a spoken response

Setup
(1) Ask students to read the speaking topic. Explain that students will work in pairs and develop and practice a role play. (2) Have students work in pairs and have them read their notes from the reading and listening tasks. Then have them complete the outlines. They may use a separate piece of paper to complete their outlines. (3) Before students continue with Step 2, remind them that they will be using the Speaking Evaluation Form on page 180 of the student book. (4) Have pairs practice their role plays. Stress that students should use ideas from the reading and listening passages, not their own ideas. (5) Have students change partners and repeat the activity. Students may use the Speaking Evaluation Form to evaluate one or both of their partners.

Expansion

After students have completed Step 3, ask for volunteers to present their role plays to the class. Give students individual feedback using the criteria on the Speaking Evaluation Form and the TOEFL iBT Integrated Speaking Task Scoring Rubric on page 235 in the student book and on page B-16 in this manual.

4 Writing

INDEPENDENT TASK

Suggested Time: 45 minutes

Focus

To give students an opportunity to produce an organized written response related to the theme of the unit using information from the unit and their own experiences

Setup

(1) Ask students to read the writing topic. Have students work on their own in Step 1. To prepare for the writing task, have students make a list of personal experiences they may have had with fraud or cheating. If they can't think of any personal experiences, they may use the experience of someone they know. Once they choose an experience, have them fill out the chart. (2) Have students work with a partner and exchange stories. Encourage them to give each other feedback. (3) Allow students to write for 20 minutes, and then remind them to use the last five minutes for proofreading and editing. The students can evaluate each other's writing using the Writing Evaluation Form on page 179 of the student book. (4) Give students feedback using the criteria on the TOEFL iBT Independent Writing Task Scoring Rubric on page 234 of the student book and page B-33 in this manual.

Expansion

If time does not allow students to complete Step 3 in class, ask them to write at home but to try to keep to the time limit.

5 Skill Focus

EXAMINATION
Suggested Time: 15 minutes

Focus

To have students examine items and tasks from the unit that focus on one essential skill assessed on the TOEFL; to reinforce a key skill that students have practiced in the unit

Setup

(1) Talk to students about what they usually do when they are reading a text in English. Ask them what they do when the come across a word or phrase that they do not understand. Most will probably say that they look the expression up in the dictionary. Others will say that they ignore it or take a guess. Explain to them that noticing context clues will help them on the TOEFL. They need to be aware of how one idea in the text may be related to other ideas. (2) Ask students to complete the Examination section. As a class, discuss their answers to the question on page 46.

Expansion

You may have students work in pairs to complete the examination section.

TIPS
Suggested Time: 10 minutes

Focus

To give students more information about the focus skill; to provide information that students can apply to related items on the TOEFL iBT

Setup

(1) Remind students that it is important to be aware of how ideas in a text are related. Tell them that there are several kinds of context clues: some are stated directly in the passage and some are inferred. (2) As a class, go through the tips together.

Expansion

Give the class a short text. Use a short reading from a class textbook or level-appropriate newspaper or magazine. Choose a few words from the texts that you think students may not know. Give the class just a few minutes to guess the definitions. Afterwards, discuss strategies the students used to find the answers.

PRACTICE
Suggested Time: 30 minutes

Focus

To have students apply the knowledge from the Skill Focus section; to help students improve their skills to learn how to use context clues to understand meaning

Setup

Review the tips for skimming and scanning with the class. Ask the students if they have any questions. Then ask them to read the directions on page 48 and complete the practice activities.

Expansion

Give students one or more short texts to read. For each text, give them a few questions to answer by identifying context clues.

Storytelling

| LISTENING |

Campus Conversation
A student talks to a professor about making an oral presentation.

Academic Listening
Interview: *Jackie Torrence*

| READING |

Review
Behind the Story of "The Metamorphosis"

| WRITING |

Integrated Task: Read, Listen, Write
Synthesize the information in the listening and reading excerpts to convey how the author, Franz Kafka, uses anthropomorphism to describe the man, Gregor Samsa.

| SPEAKING |

Independent Task
Using the concept of anthropomorphism, compare yourself to an animal, plant, or non-living thing and describe your traits and abilities.

| SKILL FOCUS |

Identifying and Using Rhetorical Structure
Identifying and using rhetorical structure means you understand the relationships among facts and ideas in different parts of a spoken or written passage.

| TOEFL® iBT TARGET SKILLS |

- Identify and express main ideas
- Identify and express details
- Make inferences
- Skim to find the structure of a passage
- Take notes and complete an outline
- Organize information to compare
- Identify different kinds of rhetorical structure

 For extra practice of TOEFL iBT skills, go to pages 208–226 of the Student Book.

1 Listening

CAMPUS CONVERSATION

PRE-LISTENING VOCABULARY
Suggested Time: 15 minutes

Focus
To acquaint students with useful vocabulary, including campus vocabulary; to aid comprehension of the conversation; to give practice inferring word meaning from context

Setup
Look at the directions as a class. Be sure each student has a partner to work with. Ask students to read each sentence with their partner and to discuss the meaning of the boldfaced words and phrases without looking at the choices below. Circulate around the room to check students' pronunciation and correct when appropriate. Encourage students to guess the meaning but make informed guesses based on the context of the sentences. Then have students complete the exercise independently. Finally, they should confirm their answers with their partners. Students can check with other pairs or the teacher if there is disagreement.

Expansion
(1) If class time is limited, you may want to assign the exercise as homework and use class time to check answers and correct pronunciation. (2) To help students memorize vocabulary, have them work in pairs to quiz each other on the definitions. (3) For homework, ask students to write one original sentence for each vocabulary item. Collect these sentences from the students in the next class. Then make a vocabulary study sheet for the students using 2 to 3 of the most exemplary sentences for each vocabulary item.

CULTURE NOTE
Suggested Time: 5 minutes

Focus
To inform students about important aspects of life at colleges and universities

Setup
Ask a student to read the Culture Note aloud. Then ask the class to brainstorm the kinds of assignments they would expect if they were to study in college. Among their responses should be exams, research papers (requiring students to investigate beyond course texts and lectures), oral presentations, group projects, and lab assignments. Ask students to discuss which assignments they prefer and why.

Expansion

Have students discuss their knowledge about the culture point in small groups or in pairs. You may want students to write a journal response, giving their views about the culture point.

FIRST LISTENING
Suggested Time: 15 minutes

Focus

To help students listen for the main ideas in a campus-based conversation

Setup

Have students read the questions before listening. Play the conversation only once. Have students take notes related to the questions as they listen. Then have students work in pairs to share notes and answer the questions.

Expansion

You may want students to wait to compare their notes about the main ideas until after they have listened a second time (during Second Listening). Then students may discuss what information helped them find *main ideas* and what information helped them find *details*.

SECOND LISTENING
Suggested Time: 25 minutes

Focus

To have students listen again, this time for details, specific information, and additional pragmatic understanding

Setup

Have students read all of the questions on their own. Stress that they should not take time to answer the questions. The purpose in reading the questions is to familiarize themselves with the questions to focus their listening. Have students review their First Listening notes to see which ideas and details they have already included. Play the conversation again. Have students add to their First Listening notes. Then have students answer the Second Listening items. Encourage them to use their notes. Finally, have students compare answers with a classmate. If they have different answers, replay the conversation rather than give the answer.

Expansion

(1) You may want to have students use their notes and their Second Listening answers to role play the conversation in pairs. Focus on the entire conversation or one particular part. Review with students pronunciation, stress, and intonation patterns. Listen to individual pairs and give feedback. (2) For homework, ask students to write one paragraph in answer to the following question: "What is your favorite or least favorite type of homework assignment and why?" When reading their responses, focus on their use of language and respond to the content as appropriate. Use the Writing Evaluation Form on page 179 of the student book and the TOEFL iBT Independent Writing Task Scoring Rubric on page 234 of the student book and page B-33 in this manual.

ACADEMIC LISTENING

FIRST LISTENING
Suggested Time: 15 minutes

Focus
To help students listen for the main ideas in an interview; to practice note taking

Setup
(1) Read the directions as a class. Ask students to look at the outline. Ask them to predict what the first three steps might be. Write their ideas on the board. Ask students to reorder the steps on the board so that they make the most sense. (2) Play the interview only once. Have students take notes to complete the information in the outline as they listen. Students may use a separate piece of paper to take notes. Then, in pairs, have students compare their outlines.

Expansion
You may want students to wait to compare their outlines until after they have finished the Second Listening. Students may discuss which information they consider is essential to include in the outline. Then students may discuss which notes they added when they listened to the interview a second time.

SECOND LISTENING
Suggested Time: 30 minutes

Focus
To have students listen again, this time for details, specific information, and pragmatic understanding

Setup
Have students read all of the questions on their own. Stress that they should not take time to answer the questions. The purpose in reading the questions is to familiarize themselves with the questions to focus their listening. Have students review their First Listening notes to see which ideas and details they have already included. Play the interview again. Have students add details to their outlines. Then have students answer the Second Listening items. Encourage them to use their notes. Finally, have students compare answers with a classmate. If they have different answers, replay the interview rather than give the answer.

Expansion
You may wish to have the class discuss storytelling. Ask students what type of storytelling they like best: listening to someone tell a story, reading a book, or seeing a movie. Alternatively, you may wish to have students write their answers to the question for homework.

ANALYSIS
Suggested Time: 15 minutes

For a discussion of Listening Analysis, please refer to Unit 2, page A-17 in this manual.

2 Reading

PRE-READING
Suggested Time: 5 minutes

Focus

To preview the reading, make predictions about the content, practice skimming and scanning skills, practice identifying rhetorical structures to answer the questions

Setup

(1) Begin by asking if anyone knows who Franz Kafka is and/or if they have heard of the story "The Metamorphosis." You might also write the title of the story on the board and ask if anyone knows the word *metamorphosis*. If no one can answer, tell them that it means *change* or *transformation*. Tell the class that "The Metamorphosis" is the story of a man, an office clerk, who changes into something else. Ask them to guess what he changes into. Turn their attention to the photograph on page 57. (2) Read the instructions as a class. After students have quickly read the text, ask them to compare their answers and report on what they have read. Note that the skill focus in this unit is identifying rhetorical structure. By answering these questions, students will, in part, be relying on this skill.

Expansion

Have pairs compare their ideas with another pair and have them combine their notes. Then have one student in each group report to the class on his/her group's ideas.

READING
Suggested Time: 45 minutes

Focus

To give practice reading for main ideas, details and inference, understanding vocabulary in context, and recognizing rhetorical style; to read a book review of "The Metamorphosis."

Setup

Have students preview the questions before they read the passage. This will help them focus their attention. Then give them 15 to 20 minutes to read and answer the questions. Have students compare their answers with a partner. If disagreements about answers arise, encourage students to review the reading text.

Expansion

(1) Encourage students to take notes as they read or to highlight important information in the margins. (2) If class time is limited, you may want to assign the reading and questions as homework and use the class time to compare and discuss answers.

3 Writing

INTEGRATED TASK: READ, LISTEN, WRITE

You many want to preview the content of the reading and listening sections by telling students that the reading excerpt presents the definition of the word *anthropomorphism* and the listening excerpt presents information about the main character in "The Metamorphosis," Gregor Samsa.

READING
Suggested Time: 30 minutes

Focus
To practice reading a short text, to practice skimming for definitions and examples

Setup
Have students read the passage and then take notes to complete the definition and examples. Students may use a separate piece of paper to take notes.

Expansion
(1) You may tell students to take notes as they read and then combine their notes with a partner's. These notes can then be shared with the class; however, eventually students will need to be able to complete these tasks efficiently on their own. (2) If class time is limited, assign the reading and note taking as homework.

LISTENING
Suggested Time: 30 minutes

Focus
To help students identify the main idea and details in a short listening passage using a graphic organizer

Setup
Before students listen, have them look at the chart and read the information. Then have them take notes to fill in the chart as they listen.

Expansion
You may want students to compare their notes in pairs or small groups. If disagreements about answers arise, play the excerpt again.

WRITING
Suggested Time: 20 minutes

Focus
To have students synthesize information from a reading text and a lecture and use the ideas in a written response

Setup

(1) Ask students to read the writing topic. Have students work in pairs and have them read their notes from the reading and listening tasks. Then have them answer the questions. (2) Before students continue with Step 2, review the Writing Evaluation Form on page 179 of the student book.

Expansion

(1) If time does not allow students to complete Step 2 in class, ask them to complete it as homework. Stress that they should take no more than 20 minutes to write, as this reflects the time constraints of the TOEFL iBT. (2) As suggested in Unit 1, you may want to include a brief activity on reported speech to help students incorporate textual information into their writing. Present common reporting verbs such as those in the list on page A-10 in the teacher's manual. (3) After students have completed Step 2, ask students to submit their writing to you. Give students individual feedback using the criteria on the Writing Evaluation Form and the TOEFL iBT Integrated Writing Task Scoring Rubric on page 233 in the student book and on page B-45 in this manual.

4 Speaking

INDEPENDENT TASK

Suggested Time: 45 minutes

Focus

To give students an opportunity to produce an organized oral response related to the theme of the unit using information from the unit and their own experiences.

Setup

Ask students to read the speaking topic. Go over the chart in Step 1 with the class to ensure that students understand what information to include. Step 2: Have students work with a partner to prepare for the speaking task. Step 3: Have students find new partners and take turns performing the speaking task. The students can evaluate each other's oral responses by using the Speaking Evaluation Form on page 180 in the student book.

Expansion

After students have completed Step 3, ask for volunteers to present their responses to the class. To assess the presentation, use the Speaking Evaluation Form on page 180 or the TOEFL iBT Independent Speaking Task Scoring Rubric on page 235 of the student book or page B-10 of this manual.

5 Skill Focus

EXAMINATION
Suggested Time: 15 minutes

Focus
To have students examine items and tasks from the unit that focus on one essential skill assessed on the TOEFL; to reinforce a key skill that students have practiced in the unit

Setup
Ask students to complete the Examination section. As a class, discuss their answers to the questions on page 64.

Expansion
To prepare for the Examination section, you may wish to give students three short readings. Each should have a different rhetorical structure (for example, a story, a description of something, an article comparing and contrasting two ideas). Ask students to talk about the differences among the texts. Point out that each text has a different rhetorical structure. Also note that that there can be more than one rhetorical structure in a single text. For example, an article about the benefits and drawbacks of owning a car (one rhetorical structure) might include a story about a person who does not own a car (narration) or a description of cars that are more environmentally friendly (description).

TIPS
Suggested Time: 10 minutes

Focus
To give students more information about the focus skill; to provide information that students can apply to related items on the TOEFL iBT

Setup
Have students read the Tips section. Then explain each tip and the example item(s) to which it refers.

Expansion
Give the students the texts you previewed in the Examination section. Are they better able to identify the rhetorical structures?

PRACTICE
Suggested Time: 30 minutes

Focus
To have students apply the knowledge from the Skill Focus section; to help students identify rhetorical structures

Setup

Review the tips for identifying rhetorical structure with the class. Ask the students if they have any questions. Then ask them to read the directions on page 67 and complete the practice activities.

Expansion

(1) For homework, give students a text from a level-appropriate English magazine or newspaper to analyze. As a class, discuss the rhetorical structure(s) used and why the author might have chosen to write in this way. (2) Ask the students to find a piece of writing from a level-appropriate English language magazine or newspaper. Have them return to class and report on the rhetorical structure(s) in the text. They may also report their findings by writing a short outline to be handed in.

Language

| LISTENING |

Campus Conversation   A student talks to a resident assistant about his accent and adjusting to life in a big city.

Academic Listening   Interview: *Speaking of Gender*

| READING |

Magazine Article   *Code Switching*

| SPEAKING |

Integrated Task: Read, Listen, Speak   Discuss the concept of stereotyping highlighted in the reading excerpt and use the example of stereotyping highlighted in the listening excerpt.

| WRITING |

Independent Task   Identify a group that has been stereotyped and support your opinion with examples.

| SKILL FOCUS |

Identifying and Using Main Ideas and Details   Identifying and using main ideas and details in listening passages and reading excerpts show that you understand a writer's or speaker's most important point about a topic.

| TOEFL® iBT TARGET SKILLS |

- Identify and express main ideas
- Identify and express details
- Make inferences
- Listen and take detailed notes
- Integrate definitions and examples
- Distinguish main ideas from details

 For extra practice of TOEFL iBT skills, go to pages 208–226 of the Student Book.

1 Listening

CAMPUS CONVERSATION

PRE-LISTENING VOCABULARY
Suggested Time: 15 minutes

Focus
To acquaint students with useful vocabulary, including campus vocabulary; to aid comprehension of the conversation; to give practice inferring word meaning from context

Setup
Look at the directions as a class. Be sure each student has a partner to work with. Ask students to read each sentence with their partner and to discuss the meaning of the boldfaced words and phrases without looking at the choices below. Circulate around the room to check students' pronunciation and correct when appropriate. Encourage students to guess the meaning but make informed guesses based on the context of the sentences. Then have students complete the exercise independently. Finally, they should confirm their answers with their partners. Students can check with other pairs or the teacher if there is disagreement.

Expansion
(1) If class time is limited, you may want to assign the exercise as homework and use class time to check answers and correct pronunciation. (2) To help students memorize vocabulary, have them work in pairs to quiz each other on the definitions. (3) For homework, ask students to write one original sentence for each vocabulary item. Collect these sentences from the students in the next class. Then make a vocabulary study sheet for the students using 2 to 3 of the most exemplary sentences for each vocabulary item.

CULTURE NOTE
Suggested Time: 5 minutes

Focus
To inform students about important aspects of life at colleges and universities

Setup
College students are expected to be fairly independent; however, there are numerous resources for students to get information and help if they need it. Part of their independence involves actively seeking out this information or help. Ask students to brainstorm what questions or needs new college students might have and where they might find the information or help they need. Write their ideas on the board.

Expansion

If possible, have students interview a Resident Assistant at a college or university and report back to the class.

FIRST LISTENING
Suggested Time: 15 minutes

Focus

To help students listen for the main ideas in a campus-based conversation

Setup

(1) Ask the class to look at the two questions. On the board make two columns: "Problem" and "Advice." Ask students to predict the student's problem(s) and the advice he will receive from the Resident Assistant. (2) Play the conversation only once. Have students take notes related to the questions as they listen. Then have students work in pairs to share notes and answer the questions.

Expansion

You may want students to wait to compare their notes about the main ideas until after they have listened a second time (during Second Listening). Then students may discuss what information helped them find *main ideas* and what information helped them find *details*.

SECOND LISTENING
Suggested Time: 25 minutes

Focus

To have students listen again, this time for details, specific information, and additional pragmatic understanding

Setup

Have students read all of the questions on their own. Stress that they should not take time to answer the questions. The purpose in reading the questions is to familiarize themselves with the questions to focus their listening. Have students review their First Listening notes to see which ideas and details they have already included. Play the conversation again. Have students add to their First Listening notes. Then have students answer the Second Listening items. Encourage them to use their notes. Finally, have students compare answers with a classmate. If they have different answers, replay the conversation rather than give the answer.

Expansion

You may want to have students use their notes and their Second Listening answers to role-play the conversation in pairs. Focus on the entire conversation or one particular part. Review with students pronunciation, stress, and intonation patterns. Listen to individual pairs and give feedback.

ACADEMIC LISTENING

FIRST LISTENING
Suggested Time: 15 minutes

Focus
To help students listen for the main ideas in an interview; to practice note taking

Setup
Read the directions as a class. Ask students to look at the charts. Ask them to predict the answers. Then play the interview. Have students complete or correct the information in the chart as they listen. Then, in pairs, have students compare their charts.

Expansion
You may want students to wait to compare their charts until after they have finished the Second Listening. Then students may discuss what information they added or corrected when they listened to the interview a second time.

SECOND LISTENING
Suggested Time: 30 minutes

Focus
To have students listen again, this time for details, specific information, and pragmatic understanding

Setup
Have students read all of the questions on their own. Stress that they should not take time to answer the questions. The purpose in reading the questions is to familiarize themselves with the questions to focus their listening. Have students review their First Listening charts to see which ideas and details they have already included. Play the interview again. Have students add details to their charts. Then have students answer the Second Listening items. Encourage them to use their notes. Finally, have students compare answers with a classmate. If they have different answers, replay the interview rather than give the answer.

Expansion
For homework, ask students to write a paragraph about how men and women in their culture use their native language differently. In the cases of some languages, the differences are more obvious. The most interesting examples will be the less obvious ones. Students might also focus on a particular word or expression that a woman might use that a man would not (or vice versa). What happens when a woman uses an expression a man typically uses or vice versa?

2 Reading

PRE-READING
Suggested Time: 5 minutes

Focus

To preview the reading, practice skimming and scanning skills, and identifying main idea and details

Setup

Note that the questions ask students to focus on the main idea and supporting details. This is the skill focus of this unit. Read the directions as a class. Have students work independently to skim the first and last sentences of each paragraph and underline them. Then have students work in pairs to answer the questions. You may want to have students use a separate piece of paper to take notes.

Expansion

(1) Have pairs compare their ideas with another pair and have them combine their notes. Then have one student in each group report to the class on his/her group's ideas. (2) Explain to students that identifying main idea and details is an important skill that will help them on the TOEFL iBT and that they will practice it again later in the unit. Have them discuss why they think this skill is important.

READING
Suggested Time: 45 minutes

Focus

To give practice reading for main ideas, details and inference, understanding vocabulary in context, and recognizing rhetorical style; to learn about code switching, a technique used by individuals who communicate with one another in more than one language

Setup

Have students preview the questions before they read the passage. This will help them focus their attention. Then give them 15 to 20 minutes to read and answer the questions. Have students compare their answers with a partner. If disagreements about answers arise, encourage students to review the reading text.

Expansion

(1) Encourage students to take notes as they read or to highlight important information in the margins. (2) If class time is limited, you may want to assign the reading and questions as homework and use class time to compare and discuss answers.

ANALYSIS
Suggested Time: 15 minutes

For a discussion of Reading Analysis, please refer to Unit 1, page A-8 in this manual.

3 Speaking

INTEGRATED TASK: READ, LISTEN, SPEAK

You many want to preview the content of the reading and listening sections by telling students that the reading excerpt defines stereotyping. In the listening excerpt a young woman interviews her friend about his accent, how people react to his accent, and how he feels about their reaction.

READING
Suggested Time: 30 minutes

Focus
To help students identify the main ideas and important details in a reading

Setup
Have students read the passage on their own and then work with a partner to complete the task.

Expansion
(1) You may tell students to take notes on a separate piece of paper as they read and then combine their notes with a partner's. These notes can then be shared with the class; however, eventually students will need to be able to complete these tasks efficiently on their own. (2) If class time is limited, assign the reading and note taking as homework.

LISTENING
Suggested Time: 30 minutes

Focus
To help students identify the main idea and details in a short listening passage; to take notes and to complete an outline

Setup
Before students listen, have them look at the outline. Explain that the (–) refers to negative comments and the (+) refers to positive comments. Then have students take notes to fill in the outline as they listen. Students may use a separate piece of paper to complete their outlines.

Expansion

You may want students to compare their notes in pairs or small groups. If disagreements about answers arise, play the excerpt again.

SPEAKING
Suggested Time: 20 minutes

Focus

To have students synthesize information from a reading text and an interview and use the ideas in a spoken response

Setup

(1) Ask students to read the speaking topic. Have students work in pairs and have them read their notes from the reading and listening tasks. Then have them complete the outlines. (2) Before students continue with Step 2, review the Speaking Evaluation Form on page 180 of the student book. (3) Have each partner give a one-minute oral response. Stress that students should use ideas from the reading and listening, not their own ideas. (4) Have students change partners and repeat the activity. Students may use the Speaking Evaluation Form to evaluate one or both of their partners.

Expansion

After students have completed Step 3, ask for volunteers to present their responses to the class. Give students individual feedback using the criteria on the Speaking Evaluation Form and the TOEFL iBT Integrated Speaking Task Scoring Rubric on page 235 in the student book and on page B-16 in this manual.

4 Writing

INDEPENDENT TASK

Suggested Time: 45 minutes

Focus

To give students an opportunity to produce an organized written response related to the theme of the unit using information from the unit and their own experiences

Setup

(1) Ask students to read the writing topic. Have students begin to work on their own and then work in a group to prepare for the writing task. Encourage students to use the discussion as an opportunity for brainstorming and to take notes during the conversation. (2) Before students write, review the Writing Evaluation Form on page 179 of the student book. (3) Allow students to write for 20 minutes, and then remind them to use the last five minutes for proofreading and editing.

Students can evaluate each other's writing using the Writing Evaluation Form. (4) Give students feedback using the criteria on the TOEFL iBT Independent Writing Task Scoring Rubric on page 234 of the student book and page B-33 in this manual.

Expansion

If time does not allow students to complete Step 2 in class, ask them to write at home but to try to keep to the time limit.

5 Skill Focus

EXAMINATION
Suggested Time: 15 minutes

Focus

To have students examine items and tasks from the unit that focus on one essential skill assessed on the TOEFL; to reinforce a key skill that students have practiced in the unit

Setup

(1) Write "Main Idea" and "Detail" in two columns on the board. Ask students to define each. Ask them to give specific examples from books, movies, or TV programs. (2) Ask students to complete the Examination section. As a class, discuss their answers to the questions on page 82.

Expansion

You may have students work in pairs to complete the Examination section.

TIPS
Suggested Time: 10 minutes

Focus

To give students more information about the focus skill; to provide information that students can apply to related items on the TOEFL iBT

Setup

Have students read the Tips section. Then explain each tip and the example item(s) it refers to. Emphasize the idea that, on the TOEFL, there is only one main idea in a passage.

Expansion

Give the class a short text. Use a short reading from a class textbook or level-appropriate newspaper or magazine. Give them some questions that require students to identify main idea and details. Give the class just a few minutes to answer the questions. Afterwards, discuss strategies the students used to find the answers.

PRACTICE
Suggested Time: 30 minutes

Focus
To have students apply the knowledge from the Skill Focus section; to help students improve their skills to identify the main idea and details

Setup
Review the tips for identifying the main idea and details with the class. Ask the students if they have any questions. Then ask them to read the directions on page 85 and complete the practice activities.

Expansion
Carefully select a passage for the class to read or listen to or a short video for them to watch. Ask them to take notes on the main idea and the details given.

Tourism

| LISTENING |

Campus Conversation — A student talks to a professor about missing a deadline for a project.

Academic Listening — Town Hall Meeting in Hyannis, Cape Cod

| READING |

Magazine Article — *Transforming a Tradition*

| WRITING |

Integrated Task: Read, Listen, Write — Summarize the points made in the lecture on the benefits of tourism to Antarctica and explain how they cast doubt on the points made in the listening excerpt on problems with tourism in Antarctica.

| SPEAKING |

Independent Task — Give your opinion on the topic of tourists visiting the long-necked women of the Padaung tribe.

| SKILL FOCUS |

Paraphrasing — Paraphrasing is the ability to restate ideas from other sources in your own words without changing the meaning.

| TOEFL® iBT TARGET SKILLS |

- Identify and express main ideas
- Identify and express details
- Make inferences
- Recognize and paraphrase speakers' opinions
- Paraphrase main ideas and details

 For extra practice of TOEFL iBT skills, go to pages 208–226 of the Student Book.

1 Listening

CAMPUS CONVERSATION

PRE-LISTENING VOCABULARY
Suggested Time: 15 minutes

Focus
To acquaint students with useful vocabulary, including campus vocabulary; to aid comprehension of the conversation; to give practice inferring word meaning from context

Setup
Look at the directions as a class. Be sure each student has a partner to work with. Ask students to read each sentence with their partner and to discuss the meaning of the boldfaced words and phrases without looking at the choices below. Circulate around the room to check students' pronunciation and correct when appropriate. Encourage students to guess the meaning but make informed guesses based on the context of the sentences. Then have students complete the exercise independently. Finally, they should confirm their answers with their partners. Students can check with other pairs or the teacher if there is disagreement.

Expansion
(1) If class time is limited, you may want to assign the exercise as homework and use class time to check answers and correct pronunciation. (2) To help students memorize vocabulary, have them work in pairs to quiz each other on the definitions. (3) For homework, ask students to write one original sentence for each vocabulary item. Collect these sentences from the students in the next class. Then make a vocabulary study sheet for the students using 2 to 3 of the most exemplary sentences for each vocabulary item.

CULTURE NOTE
Suggested Time: 5 minutes

Focus
To inform students about important aspects of life at colleges and universities

Setup
Ask the students to read the Culture Note on page 91. Answer any questions they may have about the syllabus and due dates for assignments of your course or other courses they may be taking.

Expansion

Stress that many colleges have institution-wide policies on absences but other rules, such as those relating to late work, may vary from professor to professor. Show an example of a syllabus that explains the guidelines for a class. You can use a syllabus from your own class or find a sample syllabus online.

FIRST LISTENING
Suggested Time: 15 minutes

Focus

To help students listen for the main ideas in a campus-based conversation

Setup

Have students read the questions before listening. Play the conversation only once. Have students take notes related to the questions as they listen. Then have students work in pairs to share notes and answer the questions.

Expansion

You may want students to wait to compare their notes about the main ideas until after they have listened a second time (during Second Listening). Then students may discuss what information helped them find *main ideas* and what information helped them find *details*.

SECOND LISTENING
Suggested Time: 25 minutes

Focus

To have students listen again, this time for details, specific information, and additional pragmatic understanding

Setup

Have students read all of the questions on their own. Stress that they should not take time to answer the questions. The purpose in reading the questions is to familiarize themselves with the questions to focus their listening. Have students review their First Listening notes to see which ideas and details they have already included. Play the conversation again. Have students add to their First Listening notes. Then have students answer the Second Listening items. Encourage them to use their notes. Finally, have students compare answers with a classmate. If they have different answers, replay the conversation rather than give the answer.

Expansion

You may want to model note taking for the students by playing the conversation a third time and taking notes on the board or on an overhead. Students can then compare their notes to yours, and you can discuss the differences.

ACADEMIC LISTENING

FIRST LISTENING
Suggested Time: 15 minutes

Focus
To help students listen for the main ideas in the passage; to practice note taking

Setup
(1) Tell the class that they are going to hear residents at a town meeting talk about the effect tourism has had on their town. On the board make two columns: "Benefits" and Drawbacks." Ask students to predict what they are going to hear in the listening. Write their ideas in the appropriate column. Remember that some ideas can be both a benefit and a drawback. (2) Read the directions as a class. Ask students to look at the chart. Play the passage only once. Have students take notes to complete the information in the chart as they listen. Then, in pairs, have students compare their charts.

Expansion
You may want students to wait to compare their charts until after they have finished the Second Listening. Students may discuss which information they consider is essential to include in the chart. Then students may discuss which notes they added when they listened to the passage a second time.

SECOND LISTENING
Suggested Time: 30 minutes

Focus
To have students listen again, this time for details, specific information, and pragmatic understanding

Setup
Have students read all of the questions on their own. Stress that they should not take time to answer the questions. The purpose in reading the questions is to familiarize themselves with the questions to focus their listening. Have students review their First Listening notes to see which ideas and details they have already included. Play the passage again. Have students add details to their charts. Then have students answer the Second Listening items. Encourage them to use their notes. Finally, have students compare answers with a classmate. If they have different answers, replay the passage rather than give the answer.

Expansion
(1) Ask students to work in groups to discuss the effect tourism has had on a place they know about. Encourage group members to then share their stories with the class. Have classmates evaluate each other, using the Speaking Evaluation form on page 180 in the student book. (2) This activity can also be assigned as homework in which students write a paragraph or two.

ANALYSIS
Suggested Time: 15 minutes

For a discussion of Listening Analysis, please refer to Unit 2, page A-17 in this manual.

2 Reading

PRE-READING
Suggested Time: 5 minutes

Focus

To preview the reading, practice skimming, scanning, and paraphrasing skills.

Setup

(1) Read the instructions as a class. This activity asks students to paraphrase information, the skills focus of this unit. Students should rewrite these sentences without changing the meaning. More time will be spent on paraphrasing later in the unit. (2) After students have skimmed the first sentences of each paragraph, ask them to rewrite the sentences on page 95. You may have students write on a separate piece of paper.

Expansion

Choose six students to write their sentences on the board (three students for Item 1 and three for Item 2). Discuss which sentences are closest in meaning to the ones in the passage.

READING
Suggested Time: 45 minutes

Focus

To give practice reading for main ideas, details and inference, understanding vocabulary in context, and recognizing rhetorical style; to learn about the debate over a controversial tourist attraction in Thailand

Setup

Have students preview the questions before they read the passage. This will help them focus their attention. Then give them 15 to 20 minutes to read and answer the questions. Have students compare their answers with a partner. If disagreements about answers arise, encourage students to review the reading text.

Expansion

(1) Encourage students to take notes as they read or to highlight important information in the margins. (2) If class time is limited, you may want to assign

the reading and questions as homework and use the class time to compare and discuss answers. (3) The section on analyzing reading questions appears in every other unit; however, you may want to have students analyze the question types in this unit as well.

3 Writing

INTEGRATED TASK: READ, LISTEN, WRITE

You many want to preview the content of the reading and listening sections by telling students that the reading excerpt is advertisement for travel in Antarctica. The listening excerpt presents some of the drawbacks of tourism in Antarctica.

READING
Suggested Time: 30 minutes

Focus
To help students identify the main ideas and important details in a reading

Setup
Have students read the passage on their own and then work with a partner to complete the task.

Expansion
(1) You may tell students to take notes on a separate piece of paper as they read and then combine their notes with a partner's. These notes can then be shared with the class; however, eventually students will need to be able to complete these tasks efficiently on their own. (2) If class time is limited, assign the reading and note taking as homework.

LISTENING
Suggested Time: 30 minutes

Focus
To help students identify the main idea and details in a short listening passage; to complete an outline

Setup
Before students listen, have them look at the outline and read the main idea sentence aloud. Then have them take notes to fill in the outline as they listen. Students may use a separate piece of paper to take notes.

Expansion

You may want students to compare their notes in pairs or small groups. If disagreements about answers arise, play the excerpt again.

WRITING
Suggested Time: 20 minutes

Focus

To have students synthesize information from a reading text and a listening passage and use the ideas in a written response

Setup

(1) Ask students to read the writing topic. Have them read their notes from the reading and listening tasks and complete the chart. (2) Before students continue with Step 2, review the Writing Evaluation Form on page 179 of the student book.

Expansion

If time does not allow students to complete Step 2 in class, ask them to complete it as homework. Stress that they should take no more than 20 minutes to write, as this reflects the time constraints of the TOEFL iBT.

4 Speaking

INDEPENDENT TASK

Suggested Time: 45 minutes

Focus

To give students an opportunity to participate in a debate related to the theme of the unit using information from the unit and their own opinions and experiences

Setup

(1) Ask students to read the speaking topic. Have students work in groups to prepare for the debate. (2) Before students do the speaking task, review the Speaking Evaluation Form on page 180 of the student book. (3) Have Students A and B give a two-minute oral argument for his or her position. Have Student C summarize each of the positions and choose the most convincing one. (4) Students may use the Speaking Evaluation Form to evaluate their partners.

Expansion

(1) You may wish to have students change partners and repeat the debate, making sure they are grouped with students taking the opposite position. (2) After students have completed Step 2, ask for volunteers to present their arguments to the class. Give students individual feedback using the TOEFL iBT Independent

Speaking Task Scoring Rubric on page 236 of the student book and page B-10 in this manual. Student could also audiotape their responses for homework.

5 Skill Focus

EXAMINATION
Suggested Time: 15 minutes

Focus
To have students examine items and tasks from the unit that focus on one essential skill assessed on the TOEFL; to reinforce a key skill that students have practiced in the unit

Setup
(1) Refer students back to the pre-reading activity on page 95 in the student book. Explain that rewriting a sentence in your own words is called *paraphrasing,* the skill focus of this unit. (2) Ask students to complete the Examination section. As a class, discuss their answers to the two questions on page 103.

Expansion
You may have students work in pairs to complete the Examination section.

TIPS
Suggested Time: 10 minutes

Focus
To give students more information about the focus skill; to provide information that students can apply to related items on the TOEFL iBT

Setup
Have students read the Tips section. Then explain each tip and the example item(s) it refers to.

Expansion
Note that there is a paraphrasing question in every unit of the student book. Have students review Units 1 to 5 to find paraphrasing items and review their answers.

PRACTICE
Suggested Time: 30 minutes

Focus
To have students apply the knowledge from the Skill Focus section; to help students improve their paraphrasing skills

Setup
Review the tips for paraphrasing with the class. Ask the students if they have any questions. Then ask them to read the directions on page 105 and complete the practice activities. Review their answers as a class.

Expansion
Give the class two or three quotations in English. If the quotation is not in English, they will be translating, *not* paraphrasing. Ask them to paraphrase the quotations you give them. Be sure that you can write a clear paraphrase of the quotations before you ask the students to do so.

Humor

LISTENING

Campus Conversation — A student talks to a professor about a teaching assistant's responsibilities.

Academic Listening — Lecture: *The Story of* I Love Lucy

READING

Magazine Article — *Cosby: A Different Kind of Family Show*

SPEAKING

Integrated Task: Read, Listen, Speak — Explain why the joke in the listening excerpt was funny according to the theories presented in the reading excerpt.

WRITING

Independent Task — Write about a funny TV show or movie that you enjoyed and why you thought it was funny.

SKILL FOCUS

Summarizing — Summarizing means finding the essential information from a written or spoken text, and leaving out less important details, then using this information in writing or speaking.

TOEFL® iBT TARGET SKILLS

- Identify and express main ideas
- Identify and express details
- Make inferences
- Categorize information
- Skim a reading and summarize it
- Summarize a listening and relate it to a reading
- Make an outline to prepare a summary

 For extra practice of TOEFL iBT skills, go to pages 208–226 of the Student Book.

1 Listening

CAMPUS CONVERSATION

PRE-LISTENING VOCABULARY
Suggested Time: 15 minutes

Focus
To acquaint students with useful vocabulary, including campus vocabulary; to aid comprehension of the conversation; to give practice inferring word meaning from context

Setup
Look at the directions as a class. Be sure each student has a partner to work with. Ask students to read each sentence with their partner and to discuss the meaning of the boldfaced words and phrases without looking at the choices below. Circulate around the room to check students' pronunciation and correct when appropriate. Encourage students to guess the meaning but make informed guesses based on the context of the sentences. Then have students complete the exercise independently. Finally, they should confirm their answers with their partners. Students can check with other pairs or the teacher if there is disagreement.

Expansion
(1) If class time is limited, you may want to assign the exercise as homework and use class time to check answers and correct pronunciation. (2) To help students memorize vocabulary, have them work in pairs to quiz each other on the definitions. (3) For homework, ask students to write one original sentence for each vocabulary item. Collect these sentences from the students in the next class. Then make a vocabulary study sheet for the students using 2 to 3 of the most exemplary sentences for each vocabulary item.

CULTURE NOTE
Suggested Time: 5 minutes

Focus
To inform students about important aspects of life at colleges and universities

Setup
Have students read the Culture Note on page 109. Ask them if they have had any experiences with Teaching Assistants and to share them with the class.

Expansion
If possible, invite a Teaching Assistant to your class and ask him/her to tell about his/her experiences as a Teaching Assistant.

FIRST LISTENING
Suggested Time: 15 minutes

Focus

To help students listen for the main ideas in a campus-based conversation

Setup

Have students read the questions before listening. Play the conversation only once. Have students take notes related to the questions as they listen. Then have students work in pairs to share notes and answer the questions.

Expansion

You may want students to wait to compare their notes about the main ideas until after they have listened a second time (during Second Listening). Then students may discuss what information helped them find *main ideas* and what information helped them find *details*.

SECOND LISTENING
Suggested Time: 25 minutes

Focus

To have students listen again, this time for details, specific information, and additional pragmatic understanding

Setup

Have students read all of the questions on their own. Stress that they should not take time to answer the questions. The purpose in reading the questions is to familiarize themselves with the questions to focus their listening. Have students review their First Listening notes to see which ideas and details they have already included. Play the conversation again. Have students add to their First Listening notes. Then have students answer the Second Listening items. Encourage them to use their notes. Finally, have students compare answers with a classmate. If they have different answers, replay the conversation rather than give the answer.

Expansion

Have students work in pairs to develop a conversation between the professor and the Teaching Assistant as a follow up to the Campus Conversation. Ask for volunteers to present their role plays to the class.

ACADEMIC LISTENING

FIRST LISTENING
Suggested Time: 15 minutes

Focus

To help students listen for the main ideas in a lecture; to practice note taking

Setup

(1) Read the directions as a class. Ask students to look at the chart and to focus on the information already given. Ask them to predict what kind of information they will hear. Ask, "How do you think the 'real life' of Lucille and Desi Arnaz was different from life on television?" (2) Play the lecture only once. Have students take notes to complete the information in the chart as they listen. Then, in pairs, have students compare their charts.

Expansion

You may want students to wait to compare their charts until after they have finished the Second Listening. Students may discuss which information they consider is essential to include in the chart. Then students may discuss which notes they added when they listened to the radio ads a second time.

SECOND LISTENING
Suggested Time: 30 minutes

Focus

To have students listen again, this time for details, specific information, and pragmatic understanding

Setup

Have students read all of the questions on their own. Stress that they should not take time to answer the questions. The purpose in reading the questions is to familiarize themselves with the questions to focus their listening. Have students review their First Listening notes to see which ideas and details they have already included. Play the lecture again. Have students add details to their charts. Then have students answer the Second Listening items. Encourage them to use their notes. Finally, have students compare answers with a classmate. If they have different answers, replay the lecture rather than give the answer.

Expansion

Ask students if they know of another real-life couple that worked together in television or movies. Ask them to talk about how their on-screen life was similar to or different from their real life.

2 Reading

PRE-READING
Suggested Time: 5 minutes

Focus

To preview the reading, make predictions about the content, and practice skimming, scanning, and summarizing skills

Setup

Read the directions as a class. Have students work independently to skim the first and last sentences of each paragraph and underline them. Then have students write the answer to the question. Note that the pre-reading activity asks the students to summarize what they have read. You may want to have students take notes on a separate piece of paper. Summarizing is the skill focus of this unit.

Expansion

Have students compare their answers with a partner and have them combine their notes. Then have student pairs report to the class on their ideas.

READING
Suggested Time: 45 minutes

Focus

To give practice reading for main ideas, details and inference, understanding vocabulary in context, and recognizing rhetorical style; to read an analysis of the popularity of the hit sitcom *The Cosby Show*

Setup

Have students preview the questions before they read the passage. This will help them focus their attention. Then give them 15 to 20 minutes to read and answer the questions. Have students compare their answers with a partner. If disagreements about answers arise, encourage students to review the reading text.

Expansion

(1) Encourage students to take notes as they read or to highlight important information in the margins. (2) If class time is limited, you may want to assign the reading and questions as homework and use the class time to compare and discuss answers. (3) Ask students if they have every seen *The Cosby Show* or a similar show. Ask them for their reaction.

ANALYSIS
Suggested Time: 15 minutes

For a discussion of Reading Analysis, please refer to Unit 1, page A-8 in this manual.

3 Speaking

INTEGRATED TASK: READ, LISTEN, SPEAK

You many want to preview the content of the reading and listening sections by telling students that the reading excerpt presents reasons why people find jokes funny. In the listening excerpt students hear a "lawyer joke" presented by a woman on a radio call-in show.

READING
Suggested Time: 30 minutes

Focus
To give students practice in summarizing a short text

Setup
Have students read the passage on their own and then work with a partner to complete the task.

Expansion
(1) You may tell students to take notes on a separate piece of paper as they read and then combine their notes with a partner's. These notes can then be shared with the class; however, eventually students will need to be able to complete these tasks efficiently on their own. (2) If class time is limited, assign the reading and note taking as homework.

LISTENING
Suggested Time: 30 minutes

Focus
To help students identify the main idea and details in a short listening passage; to answer questions about what they hear

Setup
Before students listen, have them look at the questions. Then have them take notes on a separate piece of paper to answer the questions as they listen.

Expansion
You may want students to compare their notes in pairs or small groups. If disagreements about answers arise, play the excerpt again.

SPEAKING
Suggested Time: 20 minutes

Focus
To have students synthesize information from a reading text and a listening passage and use the ideas in a spoken response

Setup
(1) Ask students to read the speaking topic. Have students work in pairs and have them read their notes from the reading and listening tasks. Then have them complete the outlines. (2) Before students continue with Step 2, review the Speaking Evaluation Form on page 180 of the student book. (3) Have each partner give a one-minute oral response. Stress that students should use ideas

from the reading and listening passages, not their own ideas. (4) Have students change partners and repeat the activity. Students may use the Speaking Evaluation Form to evaluate one or both of their partners.

Expansion

(1) After students have completed Step 3, ask for volunteers to present their responses to the class. Give students individual feedback using the criteria on the Speaking Evaluation Form and the TOEFL iBT Integrated Speaking Task Scoring Rubric on page 235 in the student book and on page B-16 in this manual. (2) Ask students to bring in jokes in English (they can find jokes in books or on the Internet). Then ask students to choose one they like and in groups practice telling it to each other. While student are working in groups, go around the room and check on pronunciation, stress, intonation, and pace of speaking. Allow students to share some of the funniest jokes with the class.

4 Writing

INDEPENDENT TASK

Suggested Time: 45 minutes

Focus

To give students an opportunity to produce an organized written response related to the theme of the unit using information from the unit and their own experiences

Setup

(1) Ask students to read the writing topic. Have students begin to work on their own and then work in a group to prepare for the writing task. Encourage students to use the discussion as an opportunity for brainstorming and to take notes during the conversation. (2) Before students write, review the Writing Evaluation Form on page 179 of the student book. (3) Allow students to write for 20 minutes, and then remind them to use the last five minutes for proofreading and editing. The students can evaluate each other's writing using the Writing Evaluation Form. (4) Give students feedback using the criteria on the TOEFL iBT Independent Writing Task Scoring Rubric on page 234 of the student book and page B-33 in this manual.

Expansion

If time does not allow students to complete Step 2 in class, ask them to write at home but to try to keep to the time limit.

5 Skill Focus

EXAMINATION
Suggested Time: 15 minutes

Focus
To have students examine items and tasks from the unit that focus on one essential skill assessed on the TOEFL; to reinforce a key skill that students have practiced in the unit

Setup
(1) Ask a student to tell what happened in the last movie they saw. Ask other students if they have seen this movie. Ask the first student to tell the story of the movie. Have other students who know the story fill in important points. Keep the description general. Once the general story has been told and written on the board, explain to the class that what they have just produced is a *summary*. Note that there are no extra details—just the most important points. (2) Ask students to complete the Examination section. As a class, discuss their answers to the questions on page 120.

Expansion
You may have students work in pairs to complete the Examination section.

TIPS
Suggested Time: 10 minutes

Focus
To give students more information about the focus skill; to provide information that students can apply to related items on the TOEFL iBT

Setup
Have students read the Tips section. Then explain each tip and the example item(s) to which it refers.

Expansion
Give the class a short text. Use a short reading from a class textbook or level-appropriate newspaper or magazine. Have them work in pairs to write summaries.

PRACTICE
Suggested Time: 30 minutes

Focus
To have students apply the knowledge from the Skill Focus section; to help students improve their summarizing skills

Setup
Review the tips for summarizing with the class. Ask the students if they have any questions. Then ask them to read the directions on page 122 and complete the practice activities. Review their answers as a class.

Expansion
For homework, have students write a short summary of a story they know from television, movies, the news, history, or a book they are reading in this or another class.

Fashion

| LISTENING |

Campus Conversation A student talks to a career advisor about how to dress for job interviews.

Academic Listening Interview: *Fashion in the Workplace*

| READING |

Essay *Traditional Fashion for Today's Woman*

| WRITING |

Integrated Task: Read, Listen, Write Write about the potential risks and benefits of cosmetic surgery.

| SPEAKING |

Independent Task Give your opinion on the topic of schools having a dress code or uniform policy. Include details and examples in your explanation.

| SKILL FOCUS |

Comparing and Contrasting Comparing and contrasting means recognizing relationships, analyzing similarities and differences, and distinguishing two points of view.

| TOEFL® iBT TARGET SKILLS |

- Identify and express main ideas
- Identify and express details
- Make inferences
- Categorize information
- Analyze opinions in a reading
- Discuss a position using examples

 For extra practice of TOEFL iBT skills, go to pages 208–226 of the Student Book.

1 Listening

CAMPUS CONVERSATION

PRE-LISTENING VOCABULARY
Suggested Time: 15 minutes

Focus
To acquaint students with useful vocabulary, including campus vocabulary; to aid comprehension of the conversation; to give practice inferring word meaning from context

Setup
Look at the directions as a class. Be sure each student has a partner to work with. Ask students to read each sentence with their partner and to discuss the meaning of the boldfaced words and phrases without looking at the choices below. Circulate around the room to check students' pronunciation and correct when appropriate. Encourage students to guess the meaning but make informed guesses based on the context of the sentences. Then have students complete the exercise independently. Finally, they should confirm their answers with their partners. Students can check with other pairs or the teacher if there is disagreement.

Expansion
(1) If class time is limited, you may want to assign the exercise as homework and use class time to check answers and correct pronunciation. (2) To help students memorize vocabulary, have them work in pairs to quiz each other on the definitions. (3) For homework, ask students to write one original sentence for each vocabulary item. Collect these sentences from the students in the next class. Then make a vocabulary study sheet for the students using 2 to 3 of the most exemplary sentences for each vocabulary item.

CULTURE NOTE
Suggested Time: 5 minutes

Focus
To inform students about important aspects of life at colleges and universities

Setup
Ask a student to read the Culture Note aloud. Then ask if anyone has had experiences with the career service office at a college or university.

Expansion
Have students do Internet research. Ask them to go to a college website and try to find general information about career service offices. Have them share their information in class.

FIRST LISTENING
Suggested Time: 15 minutes

Focus
To help students listen for the main ideas in a campus-based conversation

Setup
Have students read the questions before listening. Play the conversation only once. Have students take notes related to the questions as they listen. Then have students work in pairs to share notes and answer the questions.

Expansion
(1) Ask students to imagine that next week they have a job interview for a position as a teller at a local bank. Ask them how they should prepare for the interview. Ask, "What should you do to prepare for this interview?" List the students' ideas on the board. Later, if no one has mentioned it, ask: What would you wear to this interview? Why? (2) You may want students to wait to compare their notes about the main ideas until after they have listened a second time (during Second Listening). Then students may discuss what information helped them find *main ideas* and what information helped them find *details*.

SECOND LISTENING
Suggested Time: 25 minutes

Focus
To have students listen again, this time for details, specific information, and additional pragmatic understanding

Setup
Have students read all of the questions on their own. Stress that they should not take time to answer the questions. The purpose in reading the questions is to familiarize themselves with the questions to focus their listening. Have students review their First Listening notes to see which ideas and details they have already included. Play the conversation again. Have students add to their First Listening notes. Then have students answer the Second Listening items. Encourage them to use their notes. Finally, have students compare answers with a classmate. If they have different answers, replay the conversation rather than give the answer.

Expansion
Ask students to work in groups and make a list of additional questions they may have before going on job interviews. Have groups share questions with the class. Brainstorm answers.

ACADEMIC LISTENING

FIRST LISTENING
Suggested Time: 15 minutes

Focus
To help students listen for the main ideas in an interview; to practice note taking, to practice comparing and contrasting

Setup
(1) Read the directions as a class. Ask students to look at the chart. Ask them to predict what they will hear about in the interview. Note that this activity prepares students to look at two sides of an issue, an important step in comparing and contrasting information, the skill focus of this unit. (2) Play the interview only once. Have students take notes to complete the information in the chart as they listen. Then, in pairs, have students compare their charts.

Expansion
You may want students to wait to compare their charts until after they have finished the Second Listening. Students may discuss which information they consider is essential to include in the chart. Then students may discuss which notes they added when they listened to the interview a second time.

SECOND LISTENING
Suggested Time: 30 minutes

Focus
To have students listen again, this time for details, specific information, and pragmatic understanding

Setup
Have students read all of the questions on their own. Stress that they should not take time to answer the questions. The purpose in reading the questions is to familiarize themselves with the questions to focus their listening. Have students review their First Listening notes to see which ideas and details they have already included. Play the interview again. Have students add details to their charts. Then have students answer the Second Listening items. Encourage them to use their notes. Finally, have students compare answers with a classmate. If they have different answers, replay the interview rather than give the answer.

Expansion
For homework ask students to choose another profession they are interested in (or assign them a profession to investigate). Ask them to outline how they would prepare for an interview for this specific job. If time allows, you could present to students how to apply for a job, including, if appropriate, how to write a résumé (or *curriculum vitae*) and cover letter. Of course, the specifics will depend on the cultural context in which the student lives, but a résumé and cover letter are generally important for getting professional jobs.

ANALYSIS
Suggested Time: 15 minutes

For a discussion of Listening Analysis, please refer to Unit 2, page A-17 in this manual.

2 Reading

PRE-READING
Suggested Time: 5 minutes

Focus

To preview the reading, make predictions about the content, practice skimming and scanning skills, and practice comparing and contrasting information

Setup

(1) Read the directions as a class. Ask a student to describe what a sari looks like. (If no one knows, direct the class's attention to the photograph on page 132.) Then, focusing on the chart on page 131, ask students to predict the reasons *for* wearing or *for not* wearing saris they might read about in the passage. (2) Have students work independently to skim the first and last sentences of each paragraph and underline them. Then have students work in pairs to complete the chart.

Expansion

(1) Have pairs compare their ideas with another pair and have them combine their notes. Then have one student in each group report to the class on his/her group's ideas. (2) Explain to students that comparing and contrasting information is an important skill that will help them on the TOEFL iBT, and they will practice it again later in the unit. Have them discuss why they think it is important.

READING
Suggested Time: 45 minutes

Focus

To give practice reading for main ideas, details and inference, understanding vocabulary in context, and recognizing rhetorical style; to learn about how women in Sri Lanka feel about wearing saris, a traditional fashion for women

Setup

Have students preview the questions before they read the passage. This will help them focus their attention. Then give them 15 to 20 minutes to read and answer the questions. Have students compare their answers with a partner. If disagreements about answers arise, encourage students to review the reading text.

Expansion

(1) Encourage students to take notes as they read or to highlight important information in the margins. (2) If class time is limited, you may want to assign the reading and questions as homework and use the class time to compare and discuss answers. (3) If there is a comparable form of dress in the students' culture(s), focus discussion on that. Ask, "Do people still wear this fashion today?" Why and/or why not? They could discuss this fashion issue in groups and report to the class. They may also write their responses for homework.

3 Writing

INTEGRATED TASK: READ, LISTEN, WRITE

You many want to preview the content of the reading and listening sections by telling students that the reading excerpt focuses on the potential risks of cosmetic surgery. The listening excerpt focuses on some of the benefits of cosmetic surgery from a historical perspective.

READING
Suggested Time: 30 minutes

Focus
To give students practice in recognizing important details in a reading passage

Setup
Have students read the passage on their own and then work with a partner to complete the task.

Expansion
(1) You may tell students to take notes on a separate piece of paper as they read and then combine their notes with a partner's. These notes can then be shared with the class; however, eventually students will need to be able to complete these tasks efficiently on their own. (2) If class time is limited, assign the reading and note taking as homework.

LISTENING
Suggested Time: 30 minutes

Focus
To help students identify the main idea and details in a short listening passage; to answer questions about what they hear

Setup
Before students listen, have them look at the questions. Then have them take notes on a separate piece of paper to answer the questions as they listen.

Expansion

You may want students to compare their notes in pairs or small groups. If disagreements about answers arise, play the excerpt again.

WRITING
Suggested Time: 20 minutes

Focus

To have students synthesize information from a reading text and a lecture and use the ideas in a written response

Setup

(1) Ask students to read the writing topic. Have them read their notes from the reading and listening tasks and complete the chart. (2) Before students continue with Step 2, review the Writing Evaluation Form on page 179 of the student book.

Expansion

(1) If time does not allow students to complete Step 2 in class, ask them to complete it as homework. Stress that they should take no more than 20 minutes to write, as this reflects the time constraints of the TOEFL iBT. (2) After students have completed Step 2, ask students to submit their writing to you. Give students individual feedback using the criteria on the Writing Evaluation Form and the TOEFL iBT Integrated Writing Task Scoring Rubric on page 233 of the student book and on page B-45 in this manual.

4 Speaking

INDEPENDENT TASK

Suggested Time: 45 minutes

Focus

To give students an opportunity to produce an organized spoken response related to the theme of the unit using information from the unit and their own experiences

Setup

Ask students to read the speaking topic. Go over the questions in Step 1 with the class to ensure that students understand what information to include. Step 2: Have students work with a partner to complete the chart. Step 3: Have students take turns performing the speaking task. Step 4: Have students change partners and take turns giving oral responses. The students can evaluate each other's oral responses by using the Speaking Evaluation Form on page 180 of the student book.

Expansion

After students have completed Step 4, ask for volunteers to present their responses to the class. To assess the presentation, use the Speaking Evaluation Form on page 180 or the TOEFL iBT Independent Speaking Task Scoring Rubric on page 236 in the student book or page B-10 in this manual.

5 Skill Focus

EXAMINATION
Suggested Time: 15 minutes

Focus

To have students examine items and tasks from the unit that focus on one essential skill assessed on the TOEFL; to reinforce a key skill that students have practiced in the unit

Setup

(1) Remind students of the Academic Listening activity (First Listening) in which they had to identify the benefits and drawbacks of dressing down in the workplace. Explain that this is the first necessary step in comparing and contrasting: categorizing ideas. (2) Ask students to complete the Examination section. As a class, discuss their answers to the questions on the bottom of page 138.

Expansion

You may have students work in pairs to complete the examination section.

TIPS
Suggested Time: 10 minutes

Focus

To give students more information about the focus skill; to provide information that students can apply to related items on the TOEFL iBT

Setup

Have students read the Tips section. Then explain each tip and the example item(s) to which it refers.

Expansion

Look at the reading passage again. Compare and contrast the attitudes of older women in Sri Lanka with the views of younger women regarding the sari. Or compare and contrast the views of those who favor more traditional styles to those who prefer newer styles.

PRACTICE
Suggested Time: 30 minutes

Focus
To have students apply the knowledge from the Skill Focus section; to help students improve their comparing and contrasting skills

Setup
Review the tips for comparing and contrasting with the class. Ask the students if they have any questions. Then ask them to read the directions on page 140 and complete the practice activities.

Expansion
Choose an issue related to fashion or personal style relevant to your students or have them choose one. The issue may relate to cosmetic surgery, piercing, tattoos, or something else. It may be an issue that parents and younger people disagree on. There may be a debate at your school about the need for a dress code or uniforms. If the students choose their own topics (individually or in groups), be sure that their topics clearly lend themselves to comparing and contrasting. In groups of 2 to 3 students, have students outline the two sides of their argument. Then ask them to decide where they stand on the issue. Students in the same group can have different opinions. For homework tell students, "Using block or point-by-point form, write about this issue. Give both sides. Then in your conclusion, state your opinion on the issue."

Punishment

| LISTENING |

Campus Conversation — A professor talks to a student about plagiarism and academic dishonesty.

Academic Listening — Panel Discussion: *Expert Opinions on Spanking*

| READING |

Newspaper Article — *To Spank or Not to Spank?*

| SPEAKING |

Integrated Task: Read, Listen, Speak — Debate the arguments for and against the death penalty.

| WRITING |

Independent Task — Write about the proper punishment for a serious crime, such as murder.

| SKILL FOCUS |

Using Detailed Examples — Using detailed examples shows your ability to illustrate an idea and to support general statements with concrete examples.

| TOEFL® iBT TARGET SKILLS |

- Identify and express main ideas
- Identify and express details
- Make inferences
- Recognize a speaker's attitude
- Categorize opinions
- Analyze arguments
- Express an opinion using detailed examples

 For extra practice of TOEFL iBT skills, go to pages 208–226 of the Student Book.

1 Listening

CAMPUS CONVERSATION

PRE-LISTENING VOCABULARY
Suggested Time: 15 minutes

Focus
To acquaint students with useful vocabulary, including campus vocabulary; to aid comprehension of the conversation; to give practice inferring word meaning from context

Setup
Look at the directions as a class. Be sure each student has a partner to work with. Ask students to read each sentence with their partner and to discuss the meaning of the boldfaced words and phrases without looking at the choices below. Circulate around the room to check students' pronunciation and correct when appropriate. Encourage students to guess the meaning but make informed guesses based on the context of the sentences. Then have students complete the exercise independently. Finally, they should confirm their answers with their partners. Students can check with other pairs or with the teacher if there is disagreement.

Expansion
(1) If class time is limited, you may want to assign the exercise as homework and use class time to check answers and correct pronunciation. (2) To help students memorize vocabulary, have them work in pairs to quiz each other on the definitions. (3) For homework, ask students to write one original sentence for each vocabulary item. Collect these sentences from the students in the next class. Then make a vocabulary study sheet for the students using 2 to 3 of the most exemplary sentences for each vocabulary item.

CULTURE NOTE
Suggested Time: 5 minutes

Focus
To inform students about important aspects of life at colleges and universities

Setup
Ask a student to read the Culture Note aloud. Answer any questions students may have.

Expansion
(1) As a class discuss how the information in the Culture Note is similar to and/or different from the academic standards of colleges and universities in

students' home cultures. (2) You many want to bring in a copy of your school's academic honesty policy for reference and discussion.

FIRST LISTENING
Suggested Time: 15 minutes

Focus
To help students listen for the main ideas in a campus-based conversation

Setup
(1) Ask students to read the questions on page 145. Then ask them to predict what it is that the student did wrong. After writing students' ideas on the board, discuss briefly what the appropriate punishment(s) might be for each infraction. (2) Have students read the questions before listening. Play the conversation only once. Have students take notes related to the questions as they listen. Then have students work in pairs to share notes and answer the questions.

Expansion
You may want students to wait to compare their notes about the main ideas until after they have listened a second time (during Second Listening). Then students may discuss what information helped them find *main ideas* and what information helped them find *details*.

SECOND LISTENING
Suggested Time: 25 minutes

Focus
To have students listen again, this time for details, specific information, and additional pragmatic understanding

Setup
Have students read all of the questions on their own. Stress that they should not take time to answer the questions. The purpose in reading the questions is to familiarize themselves with the questions to focus their listening. Have students review their First Listening notes to see which ideas and details they have already included. Play the conversation again. Have students add to their First Listening notes. Then have students answer the Second Listening items. Encourage them to use their notes. Finally, have students compare answers with a classmate. If they have different answers, replay the conversation rather than give the answer.

Expansion
You may want to have students use their notes and their Second Listening answers to role-play the conversation in pairs. Focus on the entire conversation or one particular part. Review with students pronunciation, stress, and intonation patterns. Listen to individual pairs and give feedback.

ACADEMIC LISTENING

FIRST LISTENING
Suggested Time: 15 minutes

Focus
To help students listen for the main ideas in the listening passage; to practice note taking

Setup
(1) In the top center of the board, write the word *spanking*. Check that students know the meaning of this word. Then under the word spanking, make two columns. Label one "Arguments FOR Spanking" and label the other "Arguments AGAINST Spanking." In groups of 2 to 4 students, ask them to come up with at least three arguments on both sides of the issue. Then, as a class, discuss their ideas, noting the fact that these arguments are not always clearly black and white. There are gray areas. For example, when does a parent's touch become spanking? When does spanking actually constitute child abuse? (2) Read the directions as a class. Ask students to look at the chart on page 147. Play the listening passage only once. Have students take notes to complete the information in the chart as they listen. Then, in pairs, have students compare their charts.

Expansion
You may want students to wait to compare their charts until after they have finished the Second Listening. Students may discuss which information they consider is essential to include in the chart. Then students may discuss which notes they added when they listen to the listening passage a second time.

SECOND LISTENING
Suggested Time: 30 minutes

Focus
To have students listen again, this time for details, specific information, and pragmatic understanding

Setup
Have students read all of the questions on their own. Stress that they should not take time to answer the questions. The purpose in reading the questions is to familiarize themselves with the questions to focus their listening. Have students review their First Listening notes to see which ideas and details they have already included. Play the listening passage again. Have students add details to their charts. Then have students answer the Second Listening items. Encourage them to use their notes. Finally, have students compare answers with a classmate. If they have different answers, replay the listening passage rather than give the answer.

Expansion
You may want to have students use their notes and their Second Listening answers to prepare and record an oral summary of the panel discussion,

including the main ideas and important details that were mentioned. Have students work in small groups and share their recordings. Have group members give feedback on any important information that is missing from the summaries.

2 Reading

PRE-READING
Suggested Time: 5 minutes

Focus
To preview the reading, make predictions about the content, and practice skimming and scanning skills, to find detailed examples

Setup
Read the directions as a class. Have students work independently to skim the first sentence of each paragraph and underline them. Then have students work in pairs to brainstorm ideas and answer the questions. Note that Question 2 asks students to focus on a detailed example in support of a main idea. This is the skill focus of this unit. You may want to have students take notes on a separate piece of paper.

Expansion
(1) Have pairs compare their ideas with another pair and have them combine their notes. Then have one student in each group report to the class on his/her group's ideas. (2) Explain to students that using detailed examples is an important skill that will help them on the TOEFL iBT, and they will practice it again later in the unit. Have them discuss why they think it is important.

READING
Suggested Time: 45 minutes

Focus
To give practice reading for main ideas, details and inference, understanding vocabulary in context, and recognizing rhetorical style; to read a newspaper article that focuses on the question: Do laws about child abuse interfere with parents' ability to discipline their children?

Setup
Have students preview the questions before they read the passage. This will help them focus their attention. Then give them 15 to 20 minutes to read and answer the questions. Have students compare their answers with a partner. If disagreements about answers arise, encourage students to review the reading text.

Expansion

(1) Encourage students to take notes as they read or to highlight important information in the margins. (2) If class time is limited, you may want to assign the reading and questions as homework and use the class time to compare and discuss answers.

ANALYSIS
Suggested Time: 15 minutes

For a discussion of Reading Analysis, please refer to Unit 1, page A-8 in this manual.

3 Speaking

INTEGRATED TASK: READ, LISTEN, SPEAK

You many want to preview the content of the reading and listening sections by telling students that the reading excerpt presents an argument against the death penalty. The listening excerpt presents an argument in favor of the death penalty.

READING
Suggested Time: 30 minutes

Focus

To give students practice in summarizing a short text; to identify detailed examples

Setup

Have students read the passage on their own and then work with a partner to complete the task.

Expansion

(1) You may tell students to take notes on a separate piece of paper as they read and then combine their notes with a partner's. These notes can then be shared with the class; however, eventually students will need to be able to complete these tasks efficiently on their own. (2) If class time is limited, assign the reading and note taking as homework.

LISTENING
Suggested Time: 30 minutes

Focus

To help students identify the main idea and details in a short listening passage; to complete an outline

Setup

Before students listen, have them look at the outline and read the main idea sentence aloud. Then have them take notes to fill in the outline as they listen.

Expansion

You may want students to compare their notes in pairs or small groups. If disagreements about answers arise, play the excerpt again.

SPEAKING
Suggested Time: 20 minutes

Focus

To have students synthesize information from a reading text and a lecture and use the ideas to debate an issue.

Setup

(1) Ask students to read the speaking topic. Have students work in groups to prepare for the debate. (2) Before students do the speaking task, review the Speaking Evaluation Form on page 180 of the student book. (3) Have Students A and B give a one-minute oral argument for his or her position. Have Student C summarize each of the positions and choose the most convincing one. (4) Students may use the Speaking Evaluation Form to evaluate their partners.

Expansion

(1) You may wish to have students change partners and repeat the debate, making sure they are grouped with students taking the opposite position. (2) After students have completed Step 3, ask for volunteers to present their arguments to the class. Give students individual feedback using the TOEFL iBT Integrated Speaking Task Scoring Rubric on page 235 of the student book and page B-16 in this manual. Students could also audiotape their responses for homework.

4 Writing

INDEPENDENT TASK

Suggested Time: 45 minutes

Focus

To give students an opportunity to produce an organized written response related to the theme of the unit using information from the unit and their own experiences

Setup

(1) Ask students to read the writing topic. Have students begin to work on their own and then work in a group to prepare for the writing task. Encourage

students to use the discussion as an opportunity for brainstorming and to take notes during the conversation. (2) Before students write, review the Writing Evaluation Form on page 179 in the student book. (3) Allow students to write for 20 minutes, and then remind them to use the last five minutes for proofreading and editing. The students can evaluate each other's writing using the Writing Evaluation Form. (4) Give students feedback using the criteria on the TOEFL iBT Independent Writing Task Scoring Rubric on page 234 of the student book and page B-33 in this manual.

Expansion

If time does not allow students to complete Step 2 in class, ask them to write at home but to try to keep to the time limit.

5 Skill Focus

EXAMINATION
Suggested Time: 15 minutes

Focus

To have students examine items and tasks from the unit that focus on one essential skill assessed on the TOEFL; to reinforce a key skill that students have practiced in the unit

Setup

Lead students in a brief discussion of an issue in their lives that can be supported with a detailed example. For example, ask them if schools should hold classes year-round (12 months). Based on their own experience or that of others, they should provide a detailed example or anecdote that *demonstrates* their point.

For example, they might be against having school all year and give an example of a student who needs to work full-time during the summer to help support his/her family. Another student might argue in favor and say how she wastes her time in the summer when she could be in school preparing for college and a competitive world.

Ask students to complete the Examination section. Have them discuss their answers to the questions on pages 157–158. Note that, unlike other units, the questions come *after* the items, rather than before them.

Expansion

You may have students work in pairs to complete the Examination section.

TIPS
Suggested Time: 10 minutes

Focus
To give students more information about the focus skill; to provide information that students can apply to related items on the TOEFL iBT

Setup
Have students read the Tips section. Then explain each tip and the example item(s) it refers to.

Expansion
Ask students to present a specific opinion they have and to back it up with a detailed example. Ask students to brainstorm some ideas to get them going. Tell them to be sure to state their opinion in a complete sentence. Give them 5 minutes to plan. Then have them report in groups of 3 to 4 students. Ask the groups to select the most convincing argument in their group. Have students with convincing arguments present to the class. Give feedback on speaking, as needed.

PRACTICE
Suggested Time: 30 minutes

Focus
To have students apply the knowledge from the Skill Focus section; to help students improve their skills in identifying and using detailed examples

Setup
Review the tips for identifying and using detailed examples with the class. Ask the students if they have any questions. Then ask them to read the directions on page 160 and complete the practice activities.

Expansion
For homework, ask students to write the arguments that they discussed in their groups above in the Tips section. Ask them to organize their ideas and to write their arguments in a clear, convincing paragraph or short essay. Students may exchange papers with a partner for the next class. Have partners evaluate each other's writing using the Writing Evaluation Form on page 179 of the student book.

Marriage

| LISTENING |

Campus Conversation — A student talks to a librarian about researching a report on marriage.

Academic Listening — Lecture: *Finding a Spouse*

| READING |

Letter to the Editor — *What's Wrong with Tradition?*

| WRITING |

Integrated Task: Read, Listen, Write — Summarize the points made in the reading excerpt about polygamy, society, and religion, giving support with examples from the listening excerpt about Mormons and marriage.

| SPEAKING |

Independent Task — Compare and contrast your views on marriage with the views of a partner. Highlight some of the similarities and differences.

| SKILL FOCUS |

Recognizing and Using Cohesive Devices — Cohesive devices are words and phrases that connect parts of a written or spoken text and signal how ideas are related and organized.

| TOEFL® iBT TARGET SKILLS |

- Identify and express main ideas
- Identify and express details
- Make inferences
- Categorize and compare information
- Analyze opinions
- Express an opinion

 For extra practice of TOEFL iBT skills, go to pages 208–226 of the Student Book.

1 Listening

CAMPUS CONVERSATION

PRE-LISTENING VOCABULARY
Suggested Time: 15 minutes

Focus
To acquaint students with useful vocabulary, including campus vocabulary; to aid comprehension of the conversation; to give practice inferring word meaning from context

Setup
Look at the directions as a class. Be sure each student has a partner to work with. Ask students to read each sentence with their partner and to discuss the meaning of the boldfaced words and phrases without looking at the choices below. Circulate around the room to check students' pronunciation and correct when appropriate. Encourage students to guess the meaning but make informed guesses based on the context of the sentences. Then have students complete the exercise independently. Finally, they should confirm their answers with their partners. Students can check with other pairs or the teacher if there is disagreement.

Expansion
(1) If class time is limited, you may want to assign the exercise as homework and use class time to check answers and correct pronunciation. (2) To help students memorize vocabulary, have them work in pairs to quiz each other on the definitions. (3) For homework, ask students to write one original sentence for each vocabulary item. Collect these sentences from the students in the next class. Then make a vocabulary study sheet for the students using 2 to 3 of the most exemplary sentences for each vocabulary item.

CULTURE NOTE
Suggested Time: 5 minutes

Focus
To inform students about important aspects of life at colleges and universities

Setup
(1) Ask students how they would go about finding reliable information to use in a paper they were writing for a course. Decide which type of course in advance (i.e., history, sociology, biology) depending on the interests or needs of the class. Students will likely first mention common search engines such as Google. However, try to help them see a variety of potential sources, including

those in your school and local community. (2) Have students read the Culture Note aloud.

Expansion

Have students choose a topic to research and come up with a research plan (i.e., the sources and places they might look for information.) Suggest they go to the school or community library and interview the librarian.

FIRST LISTENING
Suggested Time: 15 minutes

Focus

To help students listen for the main ideas in a campus-based conversation

Setup

Have students read the questions before listening. Play the conversation only once. Have students take notes related to the questions as they listen. Then have students work in pairs to share notes and answer the questions.

Expansion

You may want students to wait to compare their notes about the main ideas until after they have listened a second time (during Second Listening). Then students may discuss what information helped them find *main ideas* and what information helped them find *details*.

SECOND LISTENING
Suggested Time: 25 minutes

Focus

To have students listen again, this time for details, specific information, and additional pragmatic understanding

Setup

Have students read all of the questions on their own. Stress that they should not take time to answer the questions. The purpose in reading the questions is to familiarize themselves with the questions to focus their listening. Have students review their First Listening notes to see which ideas and details they have already included. Play the conversation again. Have students add to their First Listening notes. Then have students answer the Second Listening items. Encourage them to use their notes. Finally, have students compare answers with a classmate. If they have different answers, replay the conversation rather than give the answer.

Expansion

You may want to have students use their notes and their Second Listening answers to role-play the conversation in pairs. Focus on the entire conversation or one particular part. Review with students pronunciation, stress, and intonation patterns. Listen to individual pairs and give feedback.

ACADEMIC LISTENING

FIRST LISTENING
Suggested Time: 15 minutes

Focus
To help students listen for the main ideas in a lecture; to practice note taking

Setup
Read the directions as a class. Ask students to predict what they will hear about in the lecture. Play the lecture only once. Have students take notes to complete the information in the chart as they listen. Then, in pairs, have students compare their charts.

Expansion
You may want students to wait to compare their charts until after they have finished the Second Listening. Students may discuss which information they consider is essential to include in the chart. Then students may discuss which notes they added when they listened to the lecture a second time.

SECOND LISTENING
Suggested Time: 30 minutes

Focus
To have students listen again, this time for details, specific information, and pragmatic understanding

Setup
Have students read all of the questions on their own. Stress that they should not take time to answer the questions. The purpose in reading the questions is to familiarize themselves with the questions to focus their listening. Have students review their First Listening notes to see which ideas and details they have already included. Play the lecture again. Have students add details to their charts. Then have students answer the Second Listening items. Encourage them to use their notes. Finally, have students compare answers with a classmate. If they have different answers, replay the lecture rather than give the answer.

Expansion
Ask students to react to what they have heard. If they know of similar or different marriage customs, discuss these ideas as a class. Write students' ideas on the board. Give feedback on speaking as needed.

ANALYSIS
Suggested Time: 15 minutes

For a discussion of Listening Analysis, please refer to Unit 2, page A-17 in this manual.

2 Reading

PRE-READING
Suggested Time: 5 minutes

Focus

To preview the reading, make predictions about the content, and practice skimming and scanning skills; to practice recognizing cohesive devices

Setup

Read the directions as a class. Have students work independently to skim the first and last sentences of each paragraph and underline them. Then have students work in pairs to brainstorm ideas and predict the answers to the questions. You may want students to use a separate piece of paper to take notes.

Expansion

Have pairs compare their ideas with another pair and have them combine their notes. Then have one student in each group report to the class on his/her group's ideas.

READING
Suggested Time: 45 minutes

Focus

To give practice reading for main ideas, details and inference, understanding vocabulary in context, and recognizing rhetorical style; to read a letter to the editor in which a young man argues in favor of arranged marriage

Setup

Have students preview the questions before they read the passage. This will help them focus their attention. Then give them 15 to 20 minutes to read and answer the questions. Have students compare their answers with a partner. If disagreements about answers arise, encourage students to review the reading text.

Expansion

(1) Encourage students to take notes as they read or to highlight important information in the margins. (2) If class time is limited, you may want to assign the reading and questions as homework and use the class time to compare and discuss answers.

3 Writing

INTEGRATED TASK: READ, LISTEN, WRITE

You many want to preview the content of the reading and listening sections by telling students that the reading excerpt focuses on how certain religious faiths view the practice of polygamy. The listening excerpt focuses on the Mormons and their views on marriage and polygamy.

READING
Suggested Time: 30 minutes

Focus
To help students identify the main ideas and important details in a reading

Setup
Have students read the passage on their own and then work with a partner to complete the task.

Expansion
(1) You may tell students to take notes on a separate piece of paper as they read and then combine their notes with a partner's. These notes can then be shared with the class; however, eventually students will need to be able to complete these tasks efficiently on their own. (2) If class time is limited, assign the reading and note taking as homework.

LISTENING
Suggested Time: 30 minutes

Focus
To help students identify the main idea and details in a short listening passage; to take notes using a chart

Setup
Before students listen, have them look at the chart. Then have them take notes to fill in the chart as they listen.

Expansion
You may want students to compare their notes in pairs or small groups. If disagreements about answers arise, play the excerpt again.

WRITING
Suggested Time: 20 minutes

Focus

To have students synthesize information from a reading text and a lecture and use the ideas in a written response

Setup

(1) Ask students to read the writing topic. Have them read their notes from the reading and listening tasks and answer the questions. (2) Before students continue with Step 2, review the Writing Evaluation Form on page 179 of the student book.

Expansion

(1) If time does not allow students to complete Step 2 in class, ask them to complete it as homework. Stress that they should take no more than 20 minutes to write, as this reflects the time constraints of the TOEFL iBT. (2) After students have completed Step 2, ask students to submit their writing to you. Give students individual feedback using the criteria on the Writing Evaluation Form and the TOEFL iBT Integrated Writing Task Scoring Rubric on page 233 of the student book and page B-45 in this manual.

4 Speaking

INDEPENDENT TASK

Suggested Time: 45 minutes

Focus

To give students an opportunity to produce an organized spoken response related to the theme of the unit using information from the unit and their own experiences

Setup

Ask students to read the speaking topic. Step 1: Have students work with a partner to complete the chart. Step 2: Have students take turns performing the speaking task. Step 3: Have students change partners and take turns giving oral responses. The students can evaluate each other's oral responses by using the Speaking Evaluation Form on page 180 of the student book.

Expansion

After students have completed Step 3, ask for volunteers to present their responses to the class. To assess the presentation, use the Speaking Evaluation Form or the TOEFL iBT Independent Speaking Task Scoring Rubric on page 236 in the student book or page B-10 in this manual.

5 Skill Focus

EXAMINATION
Suggested Time: 15 minutes

Focus
To have students examine items and tasks from the unit that focus on one essential skill assessed on the TOEFL; to reinforce a key skill that students have practiced in the unit

Setup
(1) Write the word *cohesive* on the board. Ask students the meaning. If they do not know, tell them that it refers to the joining of parts. When we are talking about cohesion, we are referring to how things, or in the case of English, *ideas* are connected. (2) Ask students to complete the Examination section. As a class, discuss their answers to the question on page 174.

Expansion
You may have students work in pairs to complete the Examination section.

TIPS
Suggested Time: 10 minutes

Focus
To give students more information about the focus skill; to provide information that students can apply to related items on the TOEFL iBT

Setup
Have students read the Tips section. Then explain each tip and the example item(s) to which it refers.

Expansion
Give the class a short text. Use a short reading from a class textbook or level-appropriate newspaper or magazine. Give them some questions, perhaps two that require recognizing cohesive devices. Give the class just a few minutes to answer the questions. Afterwards, discuss strategies the students used to find the answers.

PRACTICE
Suggested Time: 30 minutes

Focus
To have students apply the knowledge from the Skill Focus section; to help students improve skills in identifying and using cohesive devices

Setup

Review the tips for identifying and using cohesive devices with the class. Ask the students if they have any questions. Then ask them to read the directions on page 176 and complete the practice activities.

Expansion

Give students a short text to read, if possible from a book they are using in one of their classes. Choose a passage that is rich in cohesive devices. Ask students to read the text and to identify the cohesive devices in the text. Edit the passage by omitting some of the cohesive devices identified by the students. Does the sentence or passage still make sense if you omit the cohesive devices? Does the meaning change?

PART TWO

Scoring Guide and Practice Sets for TOEFL iBT Instructors

CONTENTS

Overview

This section of the *NorthStar: Building Skills for the TOEFL iBT Teacher's Manual* will help you understand how to use the scoring tools and procedures that trained raters use to score the TOEFL iBT test.

This section includes the following scoring tools to help you score the speaking and writing tasks in both parts of the *NorthStar: Building Skills for the TOEFL iBT* student book:

1. TOEFL iBT Guidelines and Scoring Rubrics to evaluate responses to speaking and writing tasks
2. Practice sets that include:
   - Authentic spoken and written "benchmark responses" at each score level
   - Additional authentic examples of student responses to allow you to practice scoring

Learning to use these scoring materials will improve your ability to evaluate your students on the speaking and writing tasks. As part of this learning process, it is important to suspend your own definitions of "high-level performance" or "low-level performance" and become very familiar with the TOEFL iBT tools and procedures.

TOEFL iBT spoken responses are scored on a 4-point scale, with 4 being the highest and 1 the lowest. Written responses are scored on a 5-point scale, with 5 being the highest score and 1 the lowest. (For both types of responses, a score of 0 is reserved for cases in which the speaker or writer makes no attempt to respond, responds in a language other than English, or gives a response that is unrelated to the topic. In rating student responses for *NorthStar: Building Skills for the TOEFL iBT,* you are unlikely to use the 0 score.)

Remember: Although the scoring criteria described in this section are not the only valid or useful criteria, they are the ones that will be used by raters when your students take TOEFL iBT.

Guidelines for Holistic Scoring

OVERVIEW OF HOLISTIC SCORING

Responses to the TOEFL iBT tasks must be scored holistically.

Holistic scoring:

- Involves the evaluation of a performance sample (written or spoken task in English)
- Looks at overall quality, effectiveness and completeness of speech, writing, and language within the time allotted
- Synthesizes and translates specific language features into a single holistic score

SCORING RUBRICS

This section of the manual includes four holistic scoring rubrics or guides to evaluate the responses:

- Independent Speaking Task Scoring Rubric (page B-10)
- Integrated Speaking Task Scoring Rubric (page B-16)
- Independent Writing Task Scoring Rubric (page B-33)
- Integrated Writing Task Scoring Rubric (page B-45)

Each rubric presents a set of criteria or descriptors of important performance features.

GENERAL PROCEDURES FOR SCORING HOLISTICALLY

1. Read the Scoring Rubrics carefully before beginning to score a sample.
2. Match the quality of the response to the criteria described in the Scoring Rubrics.
3. Refer to the benchmark responses in the Practice Sets to help anchor or confirm your judgments.
4. Remember that Scoring Rubrics represent a range of standards which are on a continuum. Therefore, some responses will appear to fall just on the line between two scores. If this happens, refer back directly to the Scoring Rubrics, the benchmark responses in the Practice Sets, and the additional information on scoring in this section. If you are not sure where a borderline response fits, it should receive the lower score.
5. In addition to the materials, use your training and your ongoing experience to make the best judgment possible.

TIPS FOR SCORING

- Don't focus on minor errors or a single weakness.
- Read and listen supportively; look for and reward what is done well rather than look for and penalize what has been done poorly or omitted.
- Score responses for clarity and coherence; do not supply meaning that is not there. Recognize the difference between meaning that is clearly implied and meaning that the reader has to supply in order for the response to make sense.
- Be accurate and fair by rating the entire response; sometimes students improve dramatically as they go on and other times responses begin well but decline afterward.
- Be aware of the limitations of time. Do not expect "perfect" or highly polished responses, even at the top score level.
- Do not judge a response by its length; some short responses are very good and some long responses are weak. It is important to judge the response according to the ideas and the development of the those ideas.
- Some responses of different quality earn the same score. Each score point represents a range of language proficiency.

Remember: Judge responses on how well the student uses language to communicate ideas and control the progression of ideas. Mastery of specific grammatical points or depth of vocabulary is not the central trait you are scoring for.

Scoring Speaking Task Responses

MATERIALS FOR SCORING SPEAKING TASK RESPONSES

The section includes the following material:

1. Six authentic sample tasks (text plus audio)

   - Two Independent Tasks
   - Two Integrated Tasks—Reading/Listening/Speaking
   - Two Integrated Tasks—Listening/Speaking

2. The TOEFL iBT Independent and Integrated Speaking Task Scoring Rubrics
3. Key Points for Scoring: a brief summary of key information that should be included in a high-level response to the Integrated Speaking Tasks.
4. Benchmark responses (audio CD) with annotations (text): A benchmark response is a student response at each score level (1, 2, 3, and 4) for each task. The annotations describe the most noticeable or salient features of the response. They also explain how the response meets the criteria for the designated score level. For example, if a score of 2 was assigned to a response, the annotation will explain why that response received a 2.
5. Practice responses: The audio CD includes three new, authentic student responses for each of the six tasks. These responses will allow you to practice scoring using the Scoring Rubric. You will be able to compare your practice scores with the official scores assigned by trained TOEFL iBT raters (page B-29).

Note: In Practice Sets 1 and 2, the audio icon— **01** —indicates the track number for tasks and responses included on the CD.

SCORING RUBRICS FOR SPEAKING TASKS (PAGES B-10 AND B-16)

The Scoring Rubrics for the Speaking Task responses include the following performance features:

<u>Delivery</u>: pace and clarity of speech including pronunciation, rhythm, intonation, rate of speech, pause structure, and fluency

Examples:

A level 4 response is marked by

- clear intonation patterns.
- ease of presentation.
- some minor grammatical problems.

A level 1 response is marked by

- fragmented speech with long pauses.
- numerous pronunciation difficulties.

Language Use: range, precision, and effectiveness of grammatical and lexical features

Examples:

A level 4 response is marked by

- control of a wide range of vocabulary items
- comfort with a variety of grammatical structures

A level 1 response is marked by:

- small range of vocabulary—vague and less precise word choices
- intended meaning that is unclear
- frequent repetitions since more words are used to convey the same meaning
- use of few grammatical structures

Topic Development: completeness and overall coherence

Examples:

A level 4 response is marked by

- clear point of view.
- well-supported reasons and explanations.
- ideas that progress smoothly and cohesively; however, responses do not have to be organized with a clear beginning, middle, and end.
- form that is easy to follow.

A level 1 response is marked by:

- few supporting details.
- hesitant and choppy presentation of ideas.
- general ideas with less elaboration.
- little relevant content.

When you are scoring, you must consider all three performance features: delivery, language use, topic development. To score at the highest level (4), a response must meet all **three** performance features at that level.

Example response:

Delivery: 4
Language Use: 4
Topic Development: 3
This response would receive a score of a 3 and **not** a 4.

However, a score of 4 (the highest score for the speaking tasks) does not have to be perfect and may include minor errors in grammar, pronunciation or topic development if they do not interfere with communication.

To score at the 3, 2, or 1 level, a response must meet a minimum of **two** of the performance criteria at that level.

TIPS FOR SCORING SPEAKING TASK RESPONSES

- Try to answer the question yourself using the specified preparation and response time. This will give you realistic — not overly high or low — expectations of the students.
- Avoid listening to a response numerous times before assigning a score. There is no evidence that multiple listenings provide more reliable scores.
- Listen carefully to each response.
- Consider the balance of the content, linguistic, and discourse features of the response before assigning a score. Do not be overly influenced by a single feature such as fluency or a specific grammar error.
- Avoid basing your score on a personal judgment of the opinions stated.

INDEPENDENT SPEAKING TASKS

The Independent Speaking Tasks measure students' speaking proficiency on a variety of familiar topics. The tasks are designed to elicit responses that draw on everyday language skills needed in an English-speaking environment.

The tasks require students to

- state and support an opinion.
- discuss personal preferences.
- make recommendations.
- explain the significance of ideas, people, objects, or events.
- use details, examples, and/or reasons in their responses.

PREPARING TO SCORE INDEPENDENT SPEAKING TASK RESPONSES

In this section, you will learn how to score Independent Speaking Task Responses. You will need to

- read the Independent Speaking Task Scoring Rubric on the next page.
- review the information about the Scoring Rubrics (page B-7).
- read the Independent Speaking Tasks in Practice Set 1.
- listen to the four benchmark responses (one for each scoring point) to the tasks.
- read the text annotations to each of the benchmark responses. You may want to discuss the responses with a colleague.

TOEFL® iBT Independent Speaking Task Scoring Rubric

Score	General Description	Delivery	Language Use	Topic Development
4	The response fulfills the demands of the task, with at most minor lapses in completeness. It is highly intelligible and exhibits sustained, coherent discourse. A response at this level is characterized by all of the following:	Generally well-paced flow (fluid expression). Speech is clear. It may include minor lapses, or minor difficulties with pronunciation or intonation patterns, which do not affect overall intelligibility.	The response demonstrates effective use of grammar and vocabulary. It exhibits a fairly high degree of automaticity with good control of basic and complex structures (as appropriate). Some minor (or systematic) errors are noticeable but do not obscure meaning.	Response is sustained and sufficient to the task. It is generally well developed and coherent; relationships between ideas are clear (or clear progression of ideas).
3	The response addresses the task appropriately, but may fall short of being fully developed. It is generally intelligible and coherent, with some fluidity of expression though it exhibits some noticeable lapses in the expression of ideas. A response at this level is characterized by at least two of the following:	Speech is generally clear, with some fluidity of expression, though minor difficulties with pronunciation, intonation, or pacing are noticeable and may require listener effort at times (though overall intelligibility is not significantly affected).	The response demonstrates fairly automatic and effective use of grammar and vocabulary, and fairly coherent expression of relevant ideas. Response may exhibit some imprecise or inaccurate use of vocabulary or grammatical structures or be somewhat limited in the range of structures used. This may affect overall fluency, but it does not seriously interfere with the communication of the message.	Response is mostly coherent and sustained and conveys relevant ideas/information. Overall development is somewhat limited, usually lacks elaboration or specificity. Relationships between ideas may at times not be immediately clear.
2	The response addresses the task, but development of the topic is limited. It contains intelligible speech, although problems with delivery and/or overall coherence occur; meaning may be obscured in places. A response at this level is characterized by at least two of the following:	Speech is basically intelligible, though listener effort is needed because of unclear articulation, awkward intonation, or choppy rhythm/pace; meaning may be obscured in places.	The response demonstrates limited range and control of grammar and vocabulary. These limitations often prevent full expression of ideas. For the most part, only basic sentence structures are used successfully and spoken with fluidity. Structures and vocabulary may express mainly simple (short) and/or general propositions, with simple or unclear connections made among them (serial listing, conjunction, juxtaposition).	The response is connected to the task, though the number of ideas presented or the development of ideas is limited. Mostly basic ideas are expressed with limited elaboration (details and support). At times relevant substance may be vaguely expressed or repetitious. Connections of ideas may be unclear.
1	The response is very limited in content and/or coherence or is only minimally connected to the task, or speech is largely unintelligible. A response at this level is characterized by at least two of the following:	Consistent pronunciation, stress, and intonation difficulties cause considerable listener effort; delivery is choppy, fragmented, or telegraphic; frequent pauses and hesitations.	Range and control of grammar and vocabulary severely limits (or prevents) expression of ideas and connections among ideas. Some low level responses may rely heavily on practiced or formulaic expressions.	Limited relevant content is expressed. The response generally lacks substance beyond expression of very basic ideas. Speaker may be unable to sustain speech to complete task and may rely heavily on repetition of the prompt.
0	Speaker makes no attempt to respond OR response is unrelated to the topic.			

PRACTICE SET 1

TASK 1: INDEPENDENT SPEAKING

This task asks the test takers to describe a person, place, object, or event familiar to them.

1. *Read the task below.*

Describe a class you have taken in school and explain why the class was important to you. Include details and examples to support your explanation.

Preparation Time: 15 seconds
Response Time: 45 seconds

Benchmark Responses and Annotations

2. *Listen to the four benchmark responses and read the annotations.*

Score 4: Annotation

The speaker is able to express her ideas fluently. She has a natural pace with little hesitation. While her native language obviously influences her pronunciation, her speech is generally clear. She uses intonation effectively to express meaning. She demonstrates good control of grammar and vocabulary. She produces a variety of structures and appropriate vocabulary with ease, with only minor grammatical errors. The response is complete and coherent. She clearly explains her choice of a favorite class and provides specific details and information to explain her choice.

Score 3: Annotation

The speaker is mostly clear and easy to understand. There is some hesitancy and choppiness, but this does not generally cause problems for the listener. She has fairly good control of grammatical structures and vocabulary. However, she does exhibit some inaccurate use of vocabulary and grammar (" . . . we have to presentate our ideas . . . ," " . . . we have done a lot . . . quite some practice . . . "), which affects overall grammatical fluency but does not seriously affect meaning for the listener. The task is complete but the development of ideas is somewhat limited. She lacks the elaboration typical of a higher-level response.

Score 2: Annotation

The speaker's pace is very slow and hesitant. He struggles with pronunciation of key words. Both the pace and problems with pronunciation at times make it difficult for the listener to follow. The speaker constructs only simple sentences or phrases with some error. Because of the slow delivery and lack of grammatical fluency, he is only able to convey a few ideas with some difficulty. The ideas conveyed are mostly vague and unsupported.

Score 1: Annotation

The speaker pronounces some words clearly but struggles to produce longer strings of speech. He has difficulty constructing meaningful phrases, pausing after nearly every word. The choppiness contributes to the difficulty listeners have in following the response. Only the most basic ideas are conveyed, and the ideas are not clearly connected. As a result, the response conveys little meaningful information.

PRACTICE

3. *Three more authentic student responses to this speaking task are included on the audio CD. Review the Independent Speaking Task Scoring Rubric on page B-10. Listen to the practice responses and record your score for each one BEFORE listening to the next response.*

PRACTICE A: Score _____

PRACTICE B: Score _____

PRACTICE C: Score _____

4. *Compare your scores with the trained TOEFL iBT raters' scores on page B-29.*

> If your scores are different from the trained raters' scores, review the Independent Speaking Task Scoring Rubric (page B-10) and the information about using the Scoring Rubrics (pages B-7). Then review the benchmark responses and annotations (page B-11).

TASK 2: INDEPENDENT SPEAKING

This task presents two possible actions, situations, or opinions and asks test takers to choose between the two and support their choice with reasons and details.

1. *Read the task below.*

Some universities require first-year students to live in dormitories on campus. Others allow students to live off-campus. Which policy do you think is better for first-year students and why? Include details and examples in your explanation.

Preparation Time: 15 seconds
Response Time: 45 seconds

Benchmark Responses and Annotations

2. *Listen to the four benchmark responses and read the annotations.*

Score 4: Annotation

In this response, the speaker provides a clear and coherent response. She is able to maintain a steady, fluid pace with little to no hesitation. Her pronunciation is very good. There is minor but noticeable first-language influence on stress and intonation patterns, but they do not obscure meaning for the listener. She demonstrates a range of vocabulary and grammar that is appropriate to the task. In general, the response is well developed. The speaker clearly states her opinion and provides several reasons for her point of view. She then explains each reason in varying degrees of detail. There is a clear progression of ideas and an ease of presentation typical of a level 4 response.

Score 3: Annotation

The speaker has some minor pronunciation problems but overall his speech is clear and fluid. He makes many systematic grammar errors (" . . . to make student live in the dorm," "I think it safe"). However, these inaccuracies do not seriously interfere with meaning. His vocabulary range does seem somewhat limited, resulting in vague or imprecise expression of ideas at times. He clearly states his opinion and provides two reasons, but his reasoning lacks detail. Also, there are some minor problems with coherence as he attempts to develop those reasons. For example, he suggests that it is "safer" for students to live in the dorm because they don't know the environment. He does not explicitly explain the link between safety and a lack of familiarity with the campus environment.

Score 2: Annotation

Although the speaker has problems pronouncing some words, most are clear and do not interfere with meaning. However, overall delivery is choppy and at times distracting for the listener (" . . . to know *long pause* about the city *long pause* and *long pause* . . . "). The speaker's limited range and control of grammar and vocabulary often result in vague, unsupported ideas (it is better to live in the dorm "because it is more easy for them to live," " . . . don't raise much problems"). While she does attempt to support her opinion, she struggles to provide sufficient support for her ideas.

Score 1: Annotation

Overall, the speaker has an extremely limited range of grammar and vocabulary and struggles to express her ideas. She is able to string together only a few words and often relies on individual words to convey meaning (" . . . students/ [re]lationships/communication so/very familiar/hmmm/cause . . . "). As a result, very little coherent content is expressed. While she is able to sustain speech for the full 45 seconds, delivery is choppy and fragmented with numerous pauses and hesitations, causing considerable listener effort.

PRACTICE

3. *Three more authentic student responses to this speaking task are included on the audio CD. Review the Independent Speaking Task Scoring Rubric on page B-10. Listen to the practice responses and record your score for each one BEFORE listening to the next response.*

 PRACTICE A: Score _____

 PRACTICE B: Score _____

PRACTICE C: Score _____

4. *Check your scores against the trained TOEFL iBT raters' scores on page B-29.*

> If your scores are different from the trained raters' scores, review the Independent Speaking Task Scoring Rubric (page B-10) and the information about the Scoring Rubrics (page B-7). Then review the benchmark responses and annotations (page B-13).

INTEGRATED SPEAKING TASKS

The Integrated Speaking Tasks measure test takers' speaking proficiency on the following two types of integrated tasks:

1. Integrated Task—Reading/Listening/Speaking
   Test takers perform three steps. They will (1) read a short passage on a topic, either campus-related or a lecture; (2) listen to a speaker talking about the same topic, either in a conversation or in an excerpt from a lecture; and (3) synthesize and summarize the information they have read and heard.
2. Integrated Task—Listening/Speaking
   Test takers perform two steps. They will (1) listen to part of a conversation or lecture; and (2) summarize the information, or summarize then express an opinion about it.

PREPARING TO SCORE INTEGRATED SPEAKING TASK RESPONSES

In this section, you will learn how to score Integrated Speaking Task Responses. You will need to

- Read the Integrated Speaking Task Scoring Rubric on the next page.
- Review the information about the Scoring Rubrics (page B-7).
- Read the Integrated Speaking Tasks in Practice Set 2.
- Listen to the four benchmark responses (one for each scoring point) to the tasks.
- Read the text annotations to each of the benchmark responses. You may want to discuss the responses with a colleague.
- Read the Key Points, a summary of the key information that should be included in a high-level response.

Remember: In scoring the integrated tasks, raters must evaluate the *accuracy and appropriateness of the content* as well as the other performance features (delivery, language use, and topic development). The Key Points section will assist you in evaluating this point.

TOEFL® iBT Integrated Speaking Task Scoring Rubric

Score	General Description	Delivery	Language Use	Topic Development
4	The response fulfills the demands of the task, with at most minor lapses in completeness. It is highly intelligible and exhibits sustained, coherent discourse. A response at this level is characterized by all of the following:	Speech is generally clear, fluid and sustained. It may include minor lapses or minor difficulties with pronunciation or intonation. Pace may vary at times as speaker attempts to recall information. Overall intelligibility remains high.	The response demonstrates good control of basic and complex grammatical structures that allow for coherent, efficient (automatic) expression of relevant ideas. Contains generally effective word choice. Though some minor (or systematic) errors or imprecise use may be noticeable, they do not require listener effort (or obscure meaning).	The response presents a clear progression of ideas and conveys the relevant information required by the task. It includes appropriate detail, though it may have minor errors or minor omissions.
3	The response addresses the task appropriately, but may fall short of being fully developed. It is generally intelligible and coherent, with some fluidity of expression, though it exhibits some noticeable lapses in the expression of ideas. A response at this level is characterized by at least two of the following:	Speech is generally clear, with some fluidity of expression, but it exhibits minor difficulties with pronunciation, intonation or pacing and may require some listener effort at times. Overall intelligibility remains good, however.	The response demonstrates fairly automatic and effective use of grammar and vocabulary, and fairly coherent expression of relevant ideas. Response may exhibit some imprecise or inaccurate use of vocabulary or grammatical structures or be somewhat limited in the range of structures used. Such limitations do not seriously interfere with the communication of the message.	The response is sustained and conveys relevant information required by the task. However, it exhibits some incompleteness, inaccuracy, lack of specificity with respect to content, or choppiness in the progression of ideas.
2	The response is connected to the task, though it may be missing some relevant information or contain inaccuracies. It contains some intelligible speech, but at times problems with intelligibility and/or overall coherence may obscure meaning. A response at this level is characterized by at least two of the following:	Speech is clear at times, though it exhibits problems with pronunciation, intonation or pacing and so may require significant listener effort. Speech may not be sustained at a consistent level throughout. Problems with intelligibility may obscure meaning in places (but not throughout).	The response is limited in the range and control of vocabulary and grammar demonstrated (some complex structures may be used, but typically contain errors). This results in limited or vague expression of relevant ideas and imprecise or inaccurate connections. Automaticity of expression may only be evident at the phrasal level.	The response conveys some relevant information but is clearly incomplete or inaccurate. It is incomplete if it omits key ideas, makes vague reference to key ideas, or demonstrates limited development of important information. An inaccurate response demonstrates misunderstanding of key ideas from the stimulus. Typically, ideas expressed may not be well connected or cohesive so that familiarity with the stimulus is necessary in order to follow what is being discussed.
1	The response is very limited in content or coherence or is only minimally connected to the task. Speech may be largely unintelligible. A response at this level is characterized by at least two of the following:	Consistent pronunciation and intonation problems cause considerable listener effort and frequently obscure meaning. Delivery is choppy, fragmented, or telegraphic. Speech contains frequent pauses and hesitations.	Range and control of grammar and vocabulary severely limits (or prevents) expression of ideas and connections among ideas. Some very low-level responses may rely on isolated words or short utterances to communicate ideas.	The response fails to provide much relevant content. Ideas that are expressed are often inaccurate, limited to vague utterances, or repetitions (including repetition of prompt).
0	Speaker makes no attempt to respond OR response is unrelated to the topic.			

PRACTICE SET 2

TASK 1: INTEGRATED SPEAKING—READING/LISTENING/SPEAKING

In this task, the test takers read a short passage about a campus-related situation, listen to a short conversation about the situation, and then answer a question about the information in the conversation and passage.

1. *Review the Reading, the Listening, and then the Speaking task.*

Reading

City University is planning to increase tuition and fees. Read the announcement about the increase from the president of City University. You will have 45 seconds to read the announcement. Begin reading now.

Announcement from the President

The university has decided to increase tuition and fees for all students by approximately 8 percent next semester. For the past five years, the tuition and fees have remained the same, but it is necessary to increase them now for several reasons. The university has many more students than we had five years ago, and we must hire additional professors to teach these students. We have also made a new commitment to research and technology and will be renovating and upgrading our laboratory facilities to better meet our students' needs.

Listening

Now listen to two students as they discuss the announcement.

Man: Great, now we have to come up with more money for next semester.

Woman: Yeah, I know, but I can see why. When I first started here, classes were so much smaller than they are now. With this many students, it's hard to get the personal attention you need ...

Man: Yeah, I guess you're right. In some classes I can't even get a seat. And I couldn't take the math course I wanted to because it was already full when I signed up.

Woman: And the other thing is, well, I am kind of worried about not being able to get a job after I graduate.

Man: Why? You're doing really well in your classes, aren't you?

Woman: I'm doing OK, but the facilities here are so limited. There are some great new experiments in microbiology that we can't even do here ... there isn't enough equipment in the laboratories, and the equipment they have is out of date. How am I going to compete for jobs with people who have practical research experience? I think the extra tuition will be a good investment.

Speaking

The woman expresses her opinion of the announcement made by the university president. State her opinion and explain the reasons she gives for holding that opinion.

Preparation Time: 30 seconds
Response Time: 60 seconds

Key Points

2. *Review these Key Points that should be included in the responses.*

- The woman agrees it is a good idea to raise tuition (and to increase spending on hiring professors and upgrading equipment).
- She believes that
  - classes are overcrowded, so students cannot get personal attention.
  - lab facilities are inadequate, so she cannot get the practical lab experience she will need to compete for a job.
- The woman's support of the increase should be connected to her criticisms of the university (the money will be used to hire more professors and to upgrade the lab facilities).

Benchmark Responses and Annotations

3. *Listen to the four benchmark responses and read the annotations.*

Score 4: Annotation

Overall, the speaker maintains a steady fluid pace with little hesitancy. Her rate of speech is a bit slow, but her speech is clear with few pronunciation problems. She demonstrates effective use of a range of grammatical structures and vocabulary. This allows her to express her ideas fairly fluently with few problems. She covers the key information from the reading and listening material although she has a minor inaccuracy. She seems to have concluded from the listening material that classes are full (rather than simply larger). But this misunderstanding does not significantly affect the overall accuracy of the response.

Score 3: Annotation

The speaker is generally clear. Interference from his native language is evident, but mispronunciations do not cause serious problems for listeners. The speaker is a bit hesitant as he pauses to construct phrases and search for appropriate vocabulary and/or ideas. As a result, the response is choppy at times. His use of language is generally good with some errors, but they do not obscure meaning. He is able to use a fair range of structures and appropriate word choices. The response is complete in that the speaker covers the key ideas from the reading and listening material. However, details and elaboration are limited. The response is short, but the information progresses fairly smoothly and clearly.

Score 2: Annotation

The speaker is rather slow and hesitant. She struggles to pronounce several key words. At times, the mispronunciations cause confusion for the listener. She struggles to construct grammatical phrases and sentences and is limited to very basic constructions and the present tense. There are noticeable errors of agreement and word form (" . . . a lot of thing is outdate . . . "). At times, imprecise word choice results in the vague expression of ideas. Despite her struggles, she is able to sustain speech for 60 seconds and convey key ideas from the reading and listening material. However, numerous errors at times obscure meaning and make it difficult for the listener to follow.

Score 1: Annotation

The speaker has consistent pronunciation problems, which makes it difficult to understand what he is saying most of the time. For the most part, the response is delivered one word at a time. Extremely limited grammar and vocabulary make it difficult for him to express ideas. As a result, very little coherent content is expressed.

PRACTICE

4. *Three more authentic student responses to this speaking task are included on the audio CD. Review the Integrated Speaking Task Scoring Rubric on page B-16. Listen to the practice responses and record your score for each one BEFORE listening to the next response.*

 PRACTICE A: Score _____

 PRACTICE B: Score _____

PRACTICE C: Score _____

5. *Check your scores against the trained TOEFL iBT raters' scores on page B-29.*

If your scores are different from the trained raters' scores, review the Integrated Speaking Task Scoring Rubric (page B-16) and information about the Scoring Rubrics (page B-7). Then review the benchmark responses and annotations (page B-18).

TASK 2: INTEGRATED SPEAKING—READING/LISTENING/SPEAKING

In this task, the test takers read a passage on an academic topic, listen to a short excerpt from a classroom lecture on the same topic, and then are asked to integrate the information from the reading passage and lecture.

1. *Review the Reading, the Listening, and then the Speaking task.*

Reading

Now read the passage about animal domestication. You have 45 seconds to read the passage. Begin reading now.

Animal Domestication

For thousands of years, humans have been able to domesticate, or tame, many large mammals that in the wild live together in herds. Once tamed, these mammals are used for agricultural work and transportation. Yet some herd mammals are not easily domesticated.

A good indicator of an animal's suitability for domestication is how protective the animal is of its territory. *Non-territorial* animals are more easily domesticated than territorial animals because they can live close together with animals from other herds. A second indicator is that animals with a *hierarchical social structure,* in which herd members follow a leader, are easy to domesticate since a human can function as the "leader."

Listening

Now listen to part of a lecture on this topic in an ecology class.

So we've been discussing the suitability of animals for domestication . . . particularly animals that live together in herds. Now, if we take horses, for example . . . in the wild, horses live in herds that consist of one male and several females and their young. When a herd moves, the dominant male leads, with the dominant female and her young immediately behind him. The dominant female and her young are then followed immediately by the second most important female and her young, and so on. This is why domesticated horses can be harnessed one after the other in a row. They're "programmed" to follow the lead of another horse. On top of that, you often find different herds of horses in the wild occupying overlapping areas—they don't fight off other herds that enter the same territory.

But it's exactly the opposite with an animal like the uh, the antelope . . . which . . . well, antelopes are herd animals too. But unlike horses, a male antelope will fight fiercely to prevent another male from entering its territory during the breeding season, OK—very different from the behavior of horses. Try keeping a couple of male antelopes together in a small space and see what happens. Also, antelopes don't have a social hierarchy— they don't instinctively follow any leader. That makes it harder for humans to control their behavior.

Speaking

The professor describes the behavior of horses and antelope in herds. Explain how their behavior is related to their suitability for domestication.

Preparation Time: 30 seconds
Response Time: 60 seconds

Key Points

2. *Review these Key Points that should be included in the responses.*

- Horses are hierarchical in their social structure. They naturally follow a leader. Hierarchical animals will accept a human as their leader.
- Horses are not territorial, so they can live close together/don't fight other herds that enter the same territory.

- Antelopes are not hierarchical.
- Antelopes are territorial and will fight fiercely with each other.
- Application: Thus horses have the traits that make them suitable for domestication while antelopes are not suitable.

Notes: Many people carefully describe the examples but do not really sum it up in the higher-level application. There are two results of the horses' hierarchical nature: the ability to harness them together is in the lecture; the consequence for human leadership is in the reading. Few people mention them both. One method of answering is to focus on the presence of traits in the species and skip the negatives, i.e. horses are hierarchical and antelopes are territorial, without mentioning the absence of these traits in each other.

Benchmark Responses and Annotations

3. *Listen to the four benchmark responses and read the annotations.*

Score 4: Annotation

The speaker demonstrates a fairly good range of grammar and vocabulary that allow her to express ideas somewhat fluently. She does make some noticeable errors of agreement and word form and is not very successful at using new vocabulary introduced in the reading and listening material ("they understand the hierarchy of the leader of the group whereas antelope does not follow this same pattern"). While these errors do not generally interfere with meaning, they may cause temporary problems for the listener unfamiliar with the reading and listening material. Overall, her speech is a little choppy but clear, and she makes fairly good use of intonation patterns to help convey information. She covers the key information from the combined reading and listening material, with some minor omissions. While she includes a lot of detail in her response, some ideas are not fully developed. In general, she was able to complete the content requirements satisfactorily but struggled a bit with grammar and word choice with the more difficult content.

Score 3: Annotation

The speech is generally clear and well-paced. There are some minor pronunciation problems but they do not obscure meaning for the listener. The speaker shows some automaticity of expression and moderate control of grammatical structures. Vocabulary is limited and errors of word choice and word formation cause the listener confusion at times. Most errors of grammar are minor and do not present a problem for the listener. Most noticeably, the response lacks coherence. Neither intonation nor rhetorical cues are used effectively to clarify relationships among ideas, resulting in a somewhat "rambling" quality at times. The limited use of cohesive devices and limited vocabulary contribute to some confusion about the speaker's accuracy of content. For example, she does address the two key traits relevant to the discussion of domestication (following a leader and defending territory), yet she seems to conflate the two in supporting her position (" . . . an antelope would always attack to defend the territory . . . and the horse would not because he is just following a leader so it's easier").

Score 2: Annotation

Pronunciation is a particular problem in the response. Several key words and phrases are unintelligible, requiring considerable listener effort and ultimately causing some confusion about meaning. The speaker is very slow getting started. He makes numerous false starts and is unable to organize information coherently. He struggles to construct coherent phrases. The speaker is eventually able to demonstrate some understanding of the reading and listening material (horses are hierarchical; antelopes are not and, therefore, are difficult to domesticate), but he struggles to convey the information coherently and seems unable to elaborate further. This is largely due to limitations in vocabulary and grammar. Only familiarity with the topic allows the listener to follow what is being said.

Score 1: Annotation

The response communicates very little information. Although many words are clearly pronounced, pronunciation problems obscure the meaning of a number of words. Such difficulties are compounded by numerous hesitations and pauses, resulting in considerable listener effort being required to follow the response. The speaker exhibits insufficient control of grammar and vocabulary to communicate meaningful expressions. As a result of delivery and language use problems, the response conveys no relevant content.

PRACTICE

4. *Three more authentic student responses to this speaking task are included on the audio CD. Review the Integrated Speaking Task Scoring Rubric on page B-16. Listen to the practice responses and record your score for each one BEFORE listening to the next response.*

PRACTICE A: Score _____

PRACTICE B: Score _____

PRACTICE C: Score _____

5. *Check your scores against the trained rater's scores on page B-29.*

If your scores are different from the trained raters' scores, review the Integrated Speaking Task Scoring Rubric (page B-16) and the information about the Scoring Rubrics (page B-7). Then review the benchmark responses and annotations (page B-21).

TASK 3: INTEGRATED SPEAKING TASK—LISTENING/SPEAKING

In this task, the test taker listens to a conversation and then responds to a problem presented in the conversation.

1. *Review the Listening, and then the Speaking task.*

Listening

Now listen to a conversation between two students.

Man: Hi Lisa, how's it going?

Woman: Hi Mark. Uh, I'm OK, I guess, but my schoolwork is really stressing me out.

Man: [sympathetically] Yeah? What's wrong?

Woman: Well, I've got a paper to write, and two exams to study for. And a bunch of math problems to finish. It's just so much that I can't concentrate on any of it. I start concentrating on studying for one of my exams, and then I'm like, how long's it gonna take to finish that problem set?

Man: Sounds like you've got more work than you can handle right now. [Not wanting to sound too pushy] Have you talked to some of your professors ... you know , try to explain the problem? You could probably get an extension on your paper or on the math assignment ...

Woman: You think? It would give me a little more time to prepare for exams right now.

Man: Well, another thing that you might do ... have you tried making yourself a schedule? That's what I do when I'm feeling overwhelmed.

Woman: What does that do for you?

Man: Well, it helps you focus your energies. Make yourself a chart that shows the next few days ... the time till your stuff is due.

Woman: Uh-huh. [meaning "I'm listening"]

Man: Think about what you need to do, and when you have to do it by. Then start filling in your schedule—like, 9:00 [nine] to 11:30 [eleven-thirty] A.M., study for exam. 12:00 [twelve] to 3:00 [three], work on problem set. But don't make the time periods too long. Like, don't put in eight hours straight for studying— you'll get tired or start worrying about your other work again. But if you keep to your schedule, you'll just have to worry about one thing at a time.

Woman: [somewhat noncommittally] Yeah, that might work.

Speaking

The students discuss two possible solutions to the woman's problem. Describe the problem. Then state which of the two solutions you prefer and explain why.

Preparation Time: 20 seconds
Response Time: 60 seconds

Key Points

2. *Review these Key Points that should be included in the responses.*

- Problem: The woman has too much work (and is having difficulty concentrating on any one thing).
- Solution: Ask her professors for an extension on the paper or math assignments.
- Solution: Make a schedule for herself and write down definite time periods when she will do what work.
- Preference for solution stated, with reasons why.

Benchmark Responses and Annotations

3. *Listen to the four benchmark responses and read the annotations.*

Score 4: Annotation

The speaker is fairly fluent and easy to comprehend. There is some hesitancy or choppiness, but for the most part, this seems to occur because she searches for ideas rather than because of linguistic breakdowns. In this response, the speaker has more difficulty using effective pause structure. She has a tendency to complete one thought and immediately begin the next, without pausing in between. At times she then stops and restarts the next idea, giving a somewhat rambling quality to the response. Minor but systematic grammatical errors occur but do not interfere with overall comprehensibility. The speaker states the woman's problem clearly and with ease. Despite minor grammatical errors, she supports her opinion with fairly sophisticated reasons.

Score 3: Annotation

The speaker's delivery is generally clear and well paced. She mispronounces some key words such as "schedule" (sked il) but this generally does not cause problems for the listener. Overall intelligibility is good. The speaker's use of grammatical structures is mostly limited to basic structures (mostly compounds) with some grammatical errors. Errors are generally minor and systematic and do not interfere with the message. However, the speaker's limited vocabulary often results in vague or imprecise expression of ideas (" . . . ask for less charge of work," "make a schedule where you can get fit and you waste less time"). This occasionally causes confusion for the listener. The speaker provides some relevant information (key pieces of information about the problem and solutions), but some statements are vague and efforts to elaborate or support are weak.

Score 2: Annotation

The speaker attempts to summarize the conversation and does convey some relevant information. However, only basic ideas are expressed without elaboration or clarification. For example, the problem and solutions are explained vaguely ("she has a shortage of time" and she should "schedule herself"). Some information is inaccurate. For example, the speaker says another possible solution is to "free herself," but it is not clear what he is referring to. Overall, the pace is choppy. There are many false starts, restarts, and attempts at self-correction, which continually interrupt the flow. The speaker seems to struggle to construct even short phrases due to limited vocabulary and grammar. Pronunciation is a problem, with some words and phrases unintelligible.

Score 1: Annotation

The speaker's pronunciation shows first language interference. The lack of clear articulation and the choppy, fragmented nature of the response demand considerable listener effort. Much of the substance of the response seems to rely on single words, but since the pronunciation of those words is unclear, the intended meaning is difficult to make out. The response presents evidence of a severe limitation in vocabulary and grammar ("one solution is /uh/uh preparation to time") which prevents the clear expression of ideas. Other than a brief, almost telegraphic statement of the problem ("the problem is exam stressing"), and a vague stab at stating a solution ("one solution is/uh/uh preparation to time") there is no relevant content expressed in the response.

PRACTICE

4. *Three more authentic student responses to this speaking task are included on the audio CD. Review the Integrated Speaking Task Scoring Rubric on page B-16. Listen to the practice responses and record your score for each one BEFORE listening to the next response.*

PRACTICE A: Score _____

PRACTICE B: Score _____

PRACTICE C: Score _____

5. *Check your scores against the trained rater's scores on page B-29.*

If your scores are different from the trained raters' scores, review the Integrated Speaking Task Scoring Rubric (page B-16) and the information about the Scoring Rubrics (page B-7). Then review the benchmark responses and annotations (page B-24).

TASK 4: INTEGRATED SPEAKING TASK—LISTENING/SPEAKING

In this task, test takers listen to part of an academic lecture and then answer a question based on its content.

1. *Review the Listening, and then the Speaking task.*

Listening

Now listen to part of a talk in a United States history class.

Because the United States is such a large country, it took time for a common national culture to emerge. A hundred years ago there was very little communication among the different regions of the United States. One result of this lack of communication was that people around the United States had very little in common with one another. People in different parts of the country spoke differently, dressed differently, and behaved differently. But connections among Americans began to increase thanks to two technological innovations: the automobile and the radio.

Now, automobiles began to be mass produced in the 1920s, which meant they became less expensive and more widely available. Americans in small towns and rural communities now had the ability to travel easily to nearby cities. They could even take vacations to other parts of the country. This increased mobility that automobiles provided changed people's attitudes and created links that hadn't existed before. For example, people in small towns began to adopt behaviors, clothes, and speech that were popular in big cities or in other parts of the country.

As more Americans were purchasing cars, radio ownership was also increasing dramatically. Americans in different regions of the country began to listen to the same popular radio programs and same musical artists. People repeated things they heard on the radio—some phrases and speech patterns they heard in songs and on radio programs began to be used by people all over the United States. People also listened to news reports on the radio. So they heard the same news throughout the country, whereas in newspapers much of the news tended to be local. So radio brought Americans together by offering them shared experiences and information about events all around the country.

Speaking

Using points and examples from the talk, explain how the automobile and the radio contributed to a common culture in the United States.

Preparation Time: 20 seconds
Response Time: 60 seconds

Key Points

2. *Review these Key Points that should be included in the responses.*

- When automobiles became more widely available in the 1920s, more people were able to travel to nearby cities and take vacations to other parts of the country.
- As a result of increased contact, people's attitudes and behavior began to change. For example, people in small towns began to adopt behaviors, clothes and speech that were popular in big cities.

- Radio ownership increased at this time as well, so more people were exposed to the same popular radio programs and musical artists. This meant more people began to gain familiarity with similar information and speech patterns.

Notes: The notion of "common culture" is left rather vague in the lecture, so many responses may be vague on this as well, and just talk of common experiences. A number of respondents will emphasize the lack of common culture one hundred years ago, but that is not necessary to obtain score 4.

Benchmark Responses and Annotations

3. *Listen to the four benchmark responses and read the annotations.*

Score 4: Annotation

The speaker is generally clear and easy to understand, although at times she speaks a bit too rapidly. She demonstrates good control of a range of vocabulary and grammar. While she has some errors, she is able to create effectively with the language. She uses a variety of grammatical structures and a range of appropriate vocabulary with only minor errors. Her response is complete and detailed. She does a very good job of connecting the details coherently to the larger issue of developing a common culture.

Score 3: Annotation

The speaker's pace and intelligibility are, for the most part, good. However, occasionally she exhibits problems with pronunciation of key words which cause difficulty for the listener (" . . . automobile cause people to copy the ?? ?? of people in the large and popular cities . . . "). She is able to create language somewhat fluently, but it contains noticeable grammatical errors. Imprecise vocabulary is possibly the most noticeable weakness. At times this results in vague or unclear meaning (" . . . people . . . copy what the radio said . . . like clichés and similarities that the people began to follow . . . and this cause likes and similarities that people began to use . . . ").

Score 2: Annotation

While the speech is clear at times, the speaker struggles with pronunciation. Portions of the response are unintelligible due to mispronunciation of key words or expressions. She is able to sustain the response for 60 seconds but provides very limited content overall. Limited vocabulary and grammar make it difficult for her to clearly express her ideas. While she does include some relevant information, too often statements are vague, and ideas are incomplete and not clearly connected. Only listeners with some knowledge of the listening material can follow what is being said.

Score 1: Annotation

Understanding the speaker requires considerable listener effort throughout. Vocabulary and grammar are very limited. The speaker mainly uses phrases or single words to communicate, resulting in a list-like response (" . . . taking vacation, that's help, going see other states, that's help . . . "). Near the end, he attempts to construct longer sentences but with limited success. Overall, he provides very little coherent information.

PRACTICE

4. *Three more authentic student responses to this speaking task are included on the audio CD. Review the Integrated Speaking Task Scoring Rubric on page B-16. Listen to the practice responses and record your score for each one BEFORE listening to the next response.*

PRACTICE A: Score _____

PRACTICE B: Score _____

PRACTICE C: Score _____

5. *Check your scores against the trained TOEFL iBT raters' scores on page B-29.*

If your scores are different from the trained raters' scores, review the Integrated Speaking Task Scoring Rubric (page B-16) and the information about the Scoring Rubrics (page B-7). Then review the benchmark responses and annotations (page B-27).

TRAINED TOEFL iBT RATERS' SCORES FOR PRACTICE SETS 1 AND 2 (SPEAKING)

The scores below were assigned by trained raters in a pilot test of the TOEFL iBT given to a representative sample of TOEFL test takers. Two raters scored each response and assigned the same score to the responses.

INDEPENDENT SPEAKING

Task 1, page B-12

PRACTICE A: 4
PRACTICE B: 3
PRACTICE C: 1

Task 2, page B-14

PRACTICE A: 2
PRACTICE B: 1
PRACTICE C: 2

INTEGRATED SPEAKING

Task 1, page B-19

PRACTICE A: 1
PRACTICE B: 4
PRACTICE C: 3

Task 3, page B-25

PRACTICE A: 2
PRACTICE B: 3
PRACTICE C: 1

Task 2, page B-22

PRACTICE A: 3
PRACTICE B: 3
PRACTICE C: 4

Task 4, page B-28

PRACTICE A: 1
PRACTICE B: 4
PRACTICE C: 3

Scoring Writing Task Responses

MATERIALS FOR SCORING WRITING TASK RESPONSES

The section includes the following material:

1. Two authentic sample tasks:

   - One Independent Task
   - One Integrated Task—Reading/Listening/Speaking

2. The TOEFL iBT Independent and Integrated Writing Task Scoring Rubrics

3. Topic Notes for Scoring: a summary of key information that should be included in a high-level response to the Integrated Speaking Tasks

4. Benchmark responses with annotations (text): A benchmark response is a student response at each score level (1, 2, 3, 4, and 5) for each task. The annotations describe the most noticeable or salient features of the response. They also explain how the response meets the criteria for the designated score level. For example, if a score of 2 was assigned to a response, the annotation will explain why that response received a 2.

5. Ten Practice responses to help you learn and practice how to score writing responses using the Scoring Rubric. You will be able to compare your practice scores with the official scores assigned by trained TOEFL iBT raters (page B-56).

SCORING RUBRICS FOR INDEPENDENT AND INTEGRATED WRITING TASKS (PAGES B-33 AND B-45)

The Scoring Rubrics for the Writing Task responses include the following performance features:

1. Organization
2. Coherence
3. Unity, Progression, and Redundancy
4. Development/Elaboration
5. Specificity
6. Responsiveness/Effective response/Completeness/Accuracy/Inaccuracy
7. Meaning—general
8. Meaning—specific, for Integrated Task responses
9. Language facility/Word choice/Syntactic variety/Range of Vocabulary
10. Inconsistent facility/Infacility/Error in structure/Word choice error/Error in language use
11. Idiomatic/Unidiomatic language/Idiomaticity
12. Connection
13. Clarity/Precision/Precise/Imprecision/Imprecise

For explanations of the terms on page B-30, see More about Performance Features of Writing Task Responses, page B-56.

Examples:

A level 5 response is marked by

- an understanding of the topic and task.
- successful selection of information from lecture and reading (for Integrated Task).
- coherence and accuracy in presenting information.
- a clear organization, with explanations, examples, and/or details.
- unity, progression, and coherence.
- display of language facility.

A level 3 response is marked by

- some understanding of topic or task.
- some unity, progression, and coherence but may lack some connection to task; may lack relevant connection to reading (Integrated Task).
- possible lack of major key point from lecture (Integrated Task).
- inconsistent facility in sentence formation and word choice leading to lack of clarity.
- limited range of syntactic structure and vocabulary.

A level 1 response is marked by

- lack of organization and development.
- little or no detail, or irrelevant specifics.
- lack of understanding of topic or task.
- serious or frequent errors in sentence structures or usage.

In general, responses should be scored at the highest levels (4 or 5) if **all** the score descriptors fit the response. For example, an Independent Writing response at level 5 should

- effectively address the topic AND
- be well organized AND
- display unity, progression and coherence AND
- display consistent facility with language.

A response should be scored at one of the lower levels (3, 2, or 1) if **some** or **any** of the score descriptors noticeably fit the response. For example, an Independent Writing response at level 2 could

- be limited in development OR
- be inadequate in organization OR
- use inappropriate or insufficient examples OR
- use inappropriate words OR
- show an accumulation of errors in sentence structure.

TIPS FOR SCORING WRITING TASK RESPONSES

- Try to answer the question yourself using the specified preparation and response time. This will give you realistic—not overly high or low—expectations of the students.
- Avoid reading a response numerous times before assigning a score. There is no evidence that multiple readings provide more reliable scores.
- Read each response carefully.
- Consider the balance of the content, language, and grammatical features of the response before assigning a score. Do not be overly influenced by a single feature such as extremes of length or a specific grammar error.
- Avoid basing your score on a personal judgment of the opinions stated.

INDEPENDENT WRITING TASKS

Independent Writing tasks are designed to measure students' abilities to formulate and convey in writing a response to a question. The question asks them to state and explain their position or opinion. All the information for the response comes from the writer's own knowledge, experience, and reasoning. Students have 30 minutes to complete the task.

PREPARING TO SCORE INDEPENDENT WRITING TASK RESPONSES

In this section, you will prepare to score Independent Writing Task Responses. You will need to

- read the Independent Writing Task Scoring Rubric on the next page.
- review the information about the Scoring Rubrics (page B-30).
- read the Independent Writing Task in Practice Set 3.
- read the Topic Notes, a summary of the key information that should be included in a response.
- read the five benchmark responses (one for each scoring point) to the tasks.
- read the text annotations to each of the benchmark responses. You may want to discuss the responses with a colleague.
- practice scoring Independent Writing Task responses. Ten practice responses are included.

TOEFL® iBT Independent Writing Task Scoring Rubric

Score	Task Description
5	**An essay at this level largely accomplishes all of the following:** • effectively addresses the topic and task • is well organized and well developed, using clearly appropriate explanations, exemplifications, and/or details • displays unity, progression, and coherence • displays consistent facility in the use of language, demonstrating syntactic variety, appropriate word choice, and idiomaticity, though it may have minor lexical or grammatical errors
4	**An essay at this level largely accomplishes all of the following:** • addresses the topic and task well, though some points may not be fully elaborated • is generally well organized and well developed, using appropriate and sufficient explanations, exemplifications, and/or details • displays unity, progression, and coherence, though it may contain occasional redundancy, digression, or unclear connections • displays facility in the use of language, demonstrating syntactic variety and range of vocabulary, though it will probably have occasional noticeable minor errors in structure, word form, or use of idiomatic language that do not interfere with meaning
3	**An essay at this level is marked by one or more of the following:** • addresses the topic and task using somewhat developed explanations, exemplifications, and/or details • displays unity, progression, and coherence, though connection of ideas may be occasionally obscured • may demonstrate inconsistent facility in sentence formation and word choice that may result in lack of clarity and occasionally obscure meaning • may display accurate but limited range of syntactic structures and vocabulary
2	**An essay at this level may reveal one or more of the following weaknesses:** • limited development in response to the topic and task • inadequate organization or connection of ideas • inappropriate or insufficient exemplifications, explanations, or details to support or illustrate generalizations in response to the task • a noticeably inappropriate choice of words or word forms • an accumulation of errors in sentence structure and/or usage
1	**An essay at this level is seriously flawed by one or more of the following weaknesses:** • serious disorganization or underdevelopment • little or no detail, or irrelevant specifics, or questionable responsiveness to the task • serious and frequent errors in sentence structure or usage
0	**An essay at this level** merely copies words from the topic, rejects the topic, or is otherwise not connected to the topic, is written in a foreign language, consists of keystroke characters, or is blank.

PRACTICE SET 3

TASK: INDEPENDENT WRITING

For this task, test takers are asked to write an essay that states, explains, and supports their opinion on an issue. Essays are usually about 300 words. The essay should provide support for an opinion or choice, not just a list of personal preferences.

1. *Read the question and task below.*

Do you agree or disagree with the following statement?

Always telling the truth is the most important consideration in any relationship.

Use specific reasons and examples to support your answer.

Topic Notes

2. *Review these topic notes before reading the sample responses.*

This topic supports a variety of approaches. Some writers take issue with the assertion and elaborate on instances where to them it is appropriate to lie; typically these include white lies, lies that would hurt others, and lies in a business context (which often have more to do with not disclosing proprietary information rather than outright lying). Others take the position that lies beget more lies and undermine trust; these responses elaborate in the direction of agreeing with the assertion. Still others look at both sides of the issue, often delineating or classifying situations where they consider lying appropriate and those they consider inappropriate or more consequential.

The telling of stories—real and hypothetical—is not uncommon in responses and should not be deemed inappropriate; stories, incidents, etc., are reasonable to illustrate points of view in response to this topic.

Benchmark Responses and Annotations

3. *Read the five benchmark responses and the annotations.*

RESPONSE

DISHONESTY KILLS RELIABILITY

There are certain considerations or factors that everyone takes into account in a relationship. People may look for honesty, altruism, understanding, loyalty, being thoughtful etc! Everyone would more or less wish that the person s/he is dealing with, has some of these virtues above. Putting them in an order according to their importance, however can be very subjective and relative.

When someone asks him/herself the question "What do I consider to be the most important thing in my relationship?" the answer depends on a lot of factors such as how his/her earlier relationships were.

After stating that everyone's opinion can be different about this, for me honesty, in other words, always telling the truth is the most important consideration in a relationship. Opposite of this is inarguably lying and if someone needs to lie, either s/he is hiding something or is afraid of telling me something.

In any relationship of mine, I would wish that first of all, the person I'm dealing with is honest. Even though s/he thinks that s/he did something wrong that I wouldn't like, s/he'd better tell me the truth and not lie about it. Later on if I find out about a lie or hear the truth from someone else, that'd be much more unpleasant. In that case how can I ever believe or trust that person again? How can I ever believe that this person has enough confidence in me to forgive him/her and carry on with the relationship from there. So if I cannot trust a person anymore, if the person doesn't think I can handle the truth, there's no point to continuing that relationship.

Although I would like to see altruistic, understanding, thoughtful and loyal behavior from people, an instance of the opposite of these behaviors would not upset me as much as dishonesty would. Among all the possible behaviors, dishonesty is the only one for me that terminates how I feel about a person's reliability . Therefore honesty would be my first concern and the most important consideration in a relationship.

Score 5: Annotation

In this response the writer first approaches the topic by underscoring that one could consider a number of character traits as being important to a relationship. The writer then effectively develops an argument that it is dishonesty or unwillingness to fully disclose some bad action that, unlike other negative behaviors, cannot be forgiven and is the most important factor in destroying a relationship. Language used here is fluent, accurate, and varied enough to effectively carry the writer's progression and connection of ideas.

RESPONSE

Always telling the truth in any relationship is really the most important consideration for many reasons. I could say that when you lie to someone, this person will not trust you anymore and what is a relationship based on? Trust, confidence, so the sense of relationship is being lost. Another point is that if the true is ommited once, it will surely appear sometime, somewhere and probably in the most unexpected way, causing lots of problems for the ones involved. So, the truth is the basis for everything.

First, confidence is the most important aspect of a friendship or a marriage, or anything like that, so, once it is lost, the whole thing goes down in a way that no one can bear it. To avoid losing confidence, there is only one way, telling the truth, lying will just help throwing it away. For example, a couple decided to go out on the weekend, but the man has a party to go with his friends to where he can not take his girlfriend and then he lies to her saying that he is sick and can not go to the date. She undertands him and they do not see each other in that weekend, but he goes to the party and has much fun. Suppose on monday, the girl talks to a friend that saw him at the party and asked why did not she go with him. She found out the true and all confidence was lost, the basis for their relation is now gone and what happens next is that they break up or if they do not, he will persist on lyes and someday it will end.

What happened to this couple is very common around here and many relationships, even friends and marriages end because of something like that. Some may argue that lying once or another will not interfere anything and it is part of a relation, but I strongly disagree, the most important thing is the true, even if it is to determine the end of a relation, it must be told. There are more chances to end something lying than saying what really happened.

Score 4: Annotation

This response develops reasons why lying is a bad thing, with a first paragraph that does a bit more than just introduce, a hypothetical story in paragraph 2, and a final paragraph that entertains and quickly dismisses a possible counterargument. All this amounts to solid 4-level development of the idea. The response displays facility, though not the facility and full complexity of a 5-level response and is marked by occasional and noticeable minor errors in word form "if the true is ommited," "lying will just help throwing it away," "lying once or another," "persist on lyes."

RESPONSE

Some people believe that it is one of the most important value in many relationships to tell the truth all the time. However, it cannot be always the best choice to tell the truth in many situatioins. Sometimes white lies are indispensible to keep relationships more lively and dilightly. There are some examples to support this idea.

Firstly, in the relationships between lovers, it is often essential to compliment their lovers on their appearance and their behavior. Even though they do not think that their boyfriend or girlfriend looks good on their new shoes and new clothes, it will probably diss them by telling the truth. On the other hand, little compliments will make them confident and happy making their relationship more tight.

Secondly, parents need to encourage their children by telling lies. Even if they are doing bad work on studying or exercising, telling the truth will hurt their hearts. What they need is a little encouraging words instead of truthful words.

Thirdly, for some patients telling them their current state of their desease will probably desperate them. It is accepted publically not to let the patients know the truth. They may be able to have hope to overcome their desease without knowing the truth.

In conclusion, it is not always better to tell the truth than lies. Some lies are acceptable in terms of making people's life more profusely. Not everybody has to know the truth, and it will lead them more happier not knowing it. In these cases, white lies are worth to be regarded as a virtue of people's relationships

---

Score 3: Annotation

This response focuses on explication of instances where white lies are appropriate, according to the writer. The explanations here should be considered as "somewhat developed." There is inconsistent control of structure and vocabulary: more than minor noticeable errors in both structure and vocabulary occur, e.g. "keep relationships . . . dilightly," "will probably desperate them," "making peoples life more profusely," "it will lead them more happier not knowing it." It is useful to compare the focus and coherence of this response with that of the similar-looking but more thinly developed response that scored a 2 (next page).

RESPONSE

Recently, there is a big debate on the issue that telling the truth or not is the most important consideration in the relationship between people. For my experience, I think telling a truth is the most important consideration in people's relationship. In the following, I will illustrate my opinion by two reasons.

First of all, honest make the trust stronger between friends or colleages. As we know, if people tell a lie to others he will not be trusted.When he tell a truth, others will believe that he tells a lie.For example, a person who is honest to others, can get real help and get trust of others.

Secondly, telling a lie always makes things worse not only in work but also in family life. When somebody do something wrong in his job he should annouce his mistake to his manager. If he don't do that others may continue their jobs base on the mistake. Consequently, the work will be worse and worse.

On the contrary, sometimes it is better to tell a lie to others, such as telling a lie to a patient. As we know, the sick become worse when a cancer patient know his illness. A good way to protect their life is to tell a lie. So that many doctors will not tell the truth to a dying patient.

To sum up, people should tell the truth to maintain their relationship with other people, although sometimes people have to tell a lie. People can get trust when they are honest to others.

Score 2: Annotation

At first glance, this response looks better than it is. But it definitely should be seen as no more than a middle-range 2-level response because it demonstrates insufficient exemplification and inadequate connection of ideas. The first body paragraph asserts "honest make the trust stronger" but then seems to shift, without marking the shift and so with real problems for understanding, to try to communicate a "crying wolf" concept; then it vaguely returns to say that an honest person "can get real help and get trust of others"; this last sentence in the paragraph does not advance the progression of ideas much beyond the first sentence and certainly is not an example of the point made by the second and third sentences in the paragraph, so connections in this paragraph are tenuous. The second body paragraph announces that telling a lie makes things worse at work and at home but doesn't follow through at all on the latter. The "On the contrary" paragraph comes as a complete and unmarked surprise given the introduction that presaged two reasons why telling the truth is the most important consideration. It is useful to compare this response with the Benchmark 3 response that looks very similar on the surface but has far more internal unity and coherent development than vague and vaguely connected development displayed here.

RESPONSE

Nowadays,many people think that the people who always telling the true is the most inportant consideration in any relationship between human.but another think that is necessary to tell some lies. It is seldom to reach the same issue.I agree with the first thinking because of the following reasons.

First fo all, we all live in the realized world ,people can respect you unless you want to use correct method to communicate with other people. It is very important ,especially in business , if you want to recieve the good resulit ,you must tell the ture about your own so that gain the considement.

Secondly, if you are honest man/woman, many people may be want to make friend with you. You can have more chance to communate with other people . you may be gain more information from them.

However,sometimes we must speak some lie.for examlpe,when our relatives have heavy illness such as cancer,we couldn't telling them the ture.because that not good for their health,and may be affect their life.

In conclusion,tellingthe ture is the people good behavire .we must require most of people to tell the ture.thus,we can see the better world in our life unless we always tell the ture.

Score 1: Annotation

This response should be seen as containing serious and frequent errors in sentence structure and usage. The paragraph beginning "First fo all" is nearly incomprehensible, the intention being carried by either vague vocabulary at best and some non-words "realized world", "considement"). The second paragraph is completely vague and the third body paragraph (actually one sentence) is familiar to us as a reason, but again not well expressed and certainly underdeveloped.

PRACTICE

2. *In this practice activity, there are two series of responses for you to score. There are five responses in each series. Review the Independent Writing Task Scoring Rubric (page B-33), information about using the Scoring Rubrics (page B-30), as well as Tips for Scoring Writing Task Responses (page B-32).*

   Read the practice responses and record your score for each one BEFORE reading the next response.

Series 1

PRACTICE A

The question whether the telling of the truth is the most important consideration in any relationship between people has been discussed thousands of times. After considering the opinions of myself and other people, I will state my reason of why I think the statement is not that true below.

First of all, in the relationship of a doctor and a patient we can easily imgine the stuation. When a doctor gets the result of a patient has a disease that cannot be cured anymore. The doctor has the choice of telling him the fact or not. Normally, we say, the doctor should tell the patient his disease and his current condition to let the patient make decision of his rest life. But what if the the patient is a child? I am not familiar witht the regulation of doctors on this area, but from the sense of a normal person, we are not willing to tell a child that kind of things which is out of the child's control. Whether to tell the truth is not the most important. If the disease cannot be cured, telling the truth make little sense to the patient.

Also, the dangerous of telling truth emerges in the relationship between trade competetors can be easily observed. For example, in a bidding, it is the trade custom of the participants of keeping their highest bidding price and other business information a secret. The participants even won't ask other competetors about that kind of informaiton because they know they won't get the truth of those.

Of course, telling the truth is very important in most of normal relationships of between people. We definitely like to make friends with the people who tell truths other than the people who tell lies. But in some special circumstances, telling the truth is not that important. One of the reasons is in that circumstances, the concentration is on something else and not the information is truth or not.

Score _____

PRACTICE B

I totally agree with this statement, and I have three reasons to support the decision that I made.

First, Always telling the truth in a relationship is important becuse is a demostration of love. Exemple, if you really love the person that you are with, you will not be able to tell this person a lye or something that didn't happen.

Second, Always telling the truth in your relationship will keep it alive, I mean that it will help the person who you are dating feel very good on having you, and this person will not leave you away.

Exemple, Wuold you live your date if you know that you can count on him and he always tells you the truth? Of course not!

Third, Always telling the truth in a relationship is good to yourself because in my opinion, when you've lyed you keep feeling guilty at yourself and that can destroy your relationship. Exemple, he will notice because you will act in a different way.

To concluded, Always telling the truth in your relationship is the most beautiful thing you can ever do to your love and your romance can live forever.

Score _____

PRACTICE C

It's important to tell the truth. I disagree with that. I think we
often have to lie. It's impossible to tell always the truth because if
someone felt that it makes him/her hurt. This person might not tell the truth. We
don't want people to be hurt. We also avoid some trable
because if people always tell the truth, it's never ending so telling lie help us to trable.
In buisiness telling lie is so important because if you tell lie that another people is
happy, you can be successful so we sometimes need lie because it has a lot of advantage between people.

Score _____

PRACTICE D

I agree that always telling the truth is the most important consideration in any relationship between people. I believe that honesty develops relationships that are long-lasting, meaningful, and also that foster growth and maturity.

First, relationships based on honesty tend to be long lasting. I feel that people want to be in relationships in which they can be themselves; where they don't have to pretend they are someone else to please others. In other words, people want to be genuine and want others to be genuine with them. That requires honesty and the willingness to tell the truth - always. I would much rather prefer to have friends who are willing to be always honest with me, even when such honesty may be painful. I am fortunate to have a long-lasting relationship that has been goind on for over fifteen years. The main aspect of this friendship is that my friend and I can be brutally honest with each other.

Second, relationships based on honesty are meaningful. We all have lots of acquaintances everywhere we go, but what we really need are meaningful and relevant relationships. These are those relationships based on truth, in which I can be myself and know will be accepted by my friend. Such relationships are far more relevant than those that are based only on people-pleasing behavior. I even think it is better to have one or two meaningful real friends, than many acquaintances.

Finally, honesty produces growth and maturity. Truth-telling is painful, but the good side of it is that it makes us grow. When we have friends who are brave enough to confront us concerning our shortcomings, we actually grow, not only in terms of abandoning negative behavior, but also in humility. I have grown when my true friends have been honest in confronting me when they felt I was beahing in negative ways. It hurt at first, but after a while I realized that they had confronted me because they cared for me, and valued our friendship.

In conclusion, honesty is essential for relationships between people, especially relationships that are long-lasting, meaningful and that encourage growth.

Score _____

PRACTICE E

Whenever i recognize that my brother lies to me, i scold him and tell him lying is the worst thing. Telling the truth is very important, People get very anglly when they realize that somebody lies to them. It's gonna be a like hell, if everybody lies and doesn't believe each other. Telling the truth is very important in relationships between people. However, I don't think telling the truth is not always a good idea.

People sometimes lie for good and it called a white lie. If people lie for a good propose I don't think that's bad. For example, a family can lie to the patient who is very serious ill, so wants to give up everything. Some people said, they should tell the truth that the patient may die very soon to the patient to give him or her time to prepare his or her death. I think it makes sense, but hope is very powerful and important. If the patient doesn't have willing to be live longer and just wants give up his or her life after the patient knows about his or her serious ill, it's much better not tell the patient the truth. With hope to life, the patient live long than the doctoy said he or she could.

Also, telling the truth can make a trouble between people. For instance, if a girl tells her boy friend about her ex boyfriends to be honest with him, the boy friend may get mad. He doesn't have to know about her ex boyfriends. Even he doesn't want to know about it. Also, when your friend invists you to come to the party, and if you just don't feel going to the party, it's better you say your friend that you have a exam next week instead of saying you just don't want to go to party. The lying keep your friend feel better, and the friendship between the friend and you.

I know some people who is always telling the truth. at first time, i liked them because they are very realiable. However, they often get in trouble or hurt people's feeling by telling the truth. For keeping good relationship, you should be a faithful to people, but at the same time you should learn when you should lie.

Score _____

5. *Check your scores against the trained rater's scores on page B-56.*

If your scores are different from the trained raters' scores, review the Independent Writing Task Scoring Rubric (page B-33) and the information about the Scoring Rubrics (page B-30). Then review the benchmark responses and annotations (page B-34).

Now practice scoring five more responses in Series 2.

Series 2

PRACTICE A

Telling the truth is the most important consideration in any relationship between people once you are going to deal with this person because you first of all must trust in this person, second nobody likes to be treated as a fool, and the truth makes a solid relation perdure.

Firs of all, the trust is going to keep a relation going on with confidence and confidence is something really important and you're going to trust in a person only once. If you lose the trust in someone I think that you will never more be able to trust in this person again. Will you trust a very important value to someone that has already stolen you? I bet you won't.

Second, nobody like to be seen as a fool. It's not nice been as a glown. It's not a good sensation to be kept in lies while there many people who know the truth. Can you imagine the sensation of been betrayed? How can you look at someone's face that betrayed you? A relationship, in this way, won't be nice and trustful. Once I saw that for a relationship be solid you must trust in person at the point of let yourself fell back in the person arms. I mean, you trust that the person is going to be on your back to hold you on. It won't be possible with a person that lies to you.

The truth means that you can't lie and if you can't lie you won't be able to betray, once you won't be able to hide anything. If you can't betray you're going to have a perfect relationship. The truth is really the basis of a relationship.

As a conclusion, I think that the truth is really important in a relationship because it gives you some safety in this relationship, the sensation that you won't be betrayed..

Score _____

PRACTICE B

I disagree with the statement above. Although I admit that honesty should be one of the most important consideration in human relationship, sometimes white-lies are nec-cessary not to damage the relationship.

First, it is not good to tell someone his or her faults or defects directly. By doing so, you might feel good about telling the truth, but it could hurt the people who will listen. It is naturl that people make mistakes and not everyone is perfect. Despite those shortcom-ings, we live together by understanding each other and tolerate those errors as we could be the one who makes the same mistakes next time. By being pointed out our mistakes or things other people think abominable, such as the way we look, the clothes we wear, the way we talk and so on, we might hate the person who criticize us rather than being thankful or correcting those.

Second, it is better not to tell someone serious facts that can possibly discourage him or her. I speak this from my experience. About one year ago, my nephew got into a terri-ble car accident and the doctor said he won't be able to walk again. We were all shocked and felt desprate. However, my other nephews decided not to tell the fact to their mother as she could pass off or be shocked to generate other problems of her own. I felt guilty about not telling the truth to her, who was relieved and became hope-ful by the white-lies that her son would be okay. One year since, my nephew is getting better and his mother has been a good supporter. If we had told her the truth, she would have been so desparate that she couldn't have taken good care of her son and her own health would have been in danger.

All in all, even though honesty is obviously great virtue, "always telling the truth" is not the key to maintaining good human relationship. By refraining from telling the truth in certain occasions, we prevent other people from being hurt by the remarks.

Score _____

PRACTICE C

yes, the truth is the most important in a relationship because each person hope that the people that love talk with the true.
The sentimental relationship need building on truth yet that withou this dead.
The truth for bad or hard is better that thousand of lied that i feel better.

Score _____

PRACTICE D

The relationship between poeple is very important. It is important that people have to work together to make a better life. It is sometimes hard to keep a good relation between people. Telling the true sometimes can make people problem. In my opinion, I agree that people should always tell the true to make a good relationship beteween people but in the right time.

        People should be honest to each other ever about what they are telling. It is some time important to tell the true. The story of a boy who take care the sheaps in the field is a good example. He was a good boy, but one day when he thought that lying is fun put him in a big trouble. After he lied to people, he lost his trust made him a big problem when the wolf came. This is a good example of how bad lying is. In the way to make a good relation, people should tell the true whether it may not good in some situation, but everything can be better if people learn when they should say it in the proper time. From my experiences, I used to lost my trust because I did not tell the true. When I was young, I wanted many toys , but I did not have money. I stole people money and lied about where I got the money. One day, everyone found that I stole money and lied to everyone. No one believed me any more. After I grow up and learn that lying is not good, so I always try to tell the true. It made me feel a lot better than before. However, telling the true can make prople sometimes if people don't learn about when they should say. For example, telling the true to women can make them lose their comfident and put men in trouble sometimes.

In the conclusion, I agree that people should alway tell the true to make a good relationship ;however, I think the most important about telling the true is time. If people tell the true in the wrong time, they can be in trouble anyway. The key is tell the true in the appropiate time.

Score _____

PRACTICE E

Telling the truth is an important principle for any relationships, this I agree on. Yet, it is confronted with many difficulties which make it hard to stick to this principle at all times.

Personally, I consider a lie a major break in trust, which immediately alerts me to not trust a person ever again. Of course there are variations in severity of a lie, yet I think a minor lie is simply not necessary, a major lie is a big problem, therefor I do not accept either one.

A minor lie could be to lie to a person in a small talk about your name or the city where you are from. This is simply not necessary. Of course in our time today where identity theft is a major problem, we are cautious in the information about ourselves we share with people unknown to us. Yet, if somebody lied to me about their name, this basically makes it impossible for me to built up a relationship of trust with them, no matter how well we find out we get along. According to this, the truth always is the foundation of a healthy relationship.

If the lie occurs at a later time, it becomes the character of betrayal. I would feel betrayed of the person's trust, who is likely to misjudge my reaction or opinion on something. This indicates, that this person is not as good a friend as one may have thought before, misjudging my tolerance, leaving me confused on what may have led him or her to this misconception.

There is one aspect though, that sits on the boarderlines of a lie, but has shown to be somewhat necessary. If for example a colleague is proud on her new sweater I would find a way to say something nice like "the color looks really nice on you," so I don't have to tell that I disagree on her taste. In that situation it would be unneccessaryly painful to blurr out the naked truth and hurt the persons feelings. To a closer friend I would probably indicate a little more of my opinion if he or she asked, but here, too, it is not a lie, yet not the plain truth to hold back.

Finally, I can only repeat - yes, truth is the foundation of any relationship between people! Yet it should not be a free ticket to be rude or hurt feelings unnecessarily.

Score _____

6. *Check your scores against the trained TOEFL iBT raters' scores on page B-56.*

> If your scores are different from the trained raters' scores, review the Independent Writing Task Scoring Rubric (page B-33) and the information about the Scoring Rubrics (page B-30). Then review the benchmark responses and annotations (page B-34).

INTEGRATED WRITING TASKS

Integrated Writing tasks (Reading/Listening/Writing) require writers to combine information from two academic sources: written and spoken.

Test takers must

- present accurate content called for by the question.
- use their own organization to create necessary connections among ideas in both sources.
- write approximately 150 to 225 words and complete the task in 20 minutes.

PREPARING TO SCORE INTEGRATED WRITING TASK RESPONSES

In this section, you will learn how to score Integrated Writing Task Responses. You will need to

- read the Integrated Writing Task Scoring Rubric on the next page.
- review the information about the Scoring Rubrics (page B-30).
- read the Integrated Writing Task in Practice Set 4.
- read the Topic Notes, a summary of the key information that should be included in a response.
- read the five benchmark responses (one for each scoring point) to the tasks.
- read the text annotations to each of the benchmark responses. You may want to discuss the responses with a colleague.
- practice scoring Integrated Writing responses. Ten practice reponses are included.

TOEFL® iBT Integrated Writing Task Scoring Rubric

Score	Task Description
5	A response at this level successfully selects the important information from the lecture and coherently and accurately presents this information in relation to the relevant information presented in the reading. The response is well organized, and occasional language errors that are present do not result in inaccurate or imprecise presentation of content or connections.
4	A response at this level is generally good in selecting the important information from the lecture and in coherently and accurately presenting this information in relation to the relevant information in the reading, but it may have minor omission, inaccuracy, vagueness, or imprecision of some content from the lecture or in connection to points made in the reading. A response is also scored at this level if it has more frequent or noticeable minor language errors, as long as such usage and grammatical structures do not result in anything more than an occasional lapse of clarity or in the connection of ideas.
3	A response at this level contains some important information from the lecture and conveys some relevant connection to the reading, but it is marked by one or more of the following: • Although the overall response is definitely oriented to the task, it conveys only vague, global, unclear, or somewhat imprecise connection of the points made in the lecture to points made in the reading. • The response may omit one major key point made in the lecture. • Some key points made in the lecture or the reading, or connections between the two, may be incomplete, inaccurate, or imprecise. • Errors of usage and/or grammar may be more frequent or may result in noticeably vague expressions or obscured meanings in conveying ideas and connections.
2	A response at this level contains some relevant information from the lecture, but is marked by significant language difficulties or by significant omission or inaccuracy of important ideas from the lecture or in the connections between the lecture and the reading; a response at this level is marked by one or more of the following: • The response significantly misrepresents or completely omits the overall connection between the lecture and the reading. • The response significantly omits or significantly misrepresents important points made in the lecture. • The response contains language errors or expressions that largely obscure connections or meaning at key junctures, or that would likely obscure understanding of key ideas for a reader not already familiar with the reading and the lecture.
1	A response at this level is marked by one or more of the following: • The response provides little or no meaningful or relevant coherent content from the lecture. • The language level of the response is so low that it is difficult to derive meaning.
0	A response at this level merely copies sentences from the reading, rejects the topic or is otherwise not connected to the topic, is written in a foreign language, consists of keystroke characters, or is blank.

PRACTICE SET 4

TASK: INTEGRATED WRITING—READING/LISTENING/WRITING

For this task, test takers are asked to write a summary of important points made in an academic listening passage and explain how these relate to points made in an academic reading passage. Responses should be about 150–225 words.

1. *Read the Reading and the Listening script, then read the Writing task.*

Reading

Read the following passage for three minutes. Take notes on the passage if you wish.

In many organizations, perhaps the best way to approach certain new projects is to assemble a group of people into a team. Having a team of people attack a project offers several advantages. First of all, a group of people has a wider range of knowledge, expertise, and skills than any single individual is likely to possess. Also, because of the numbers of people involved and the greater resources they possess, a group can work more quickly in response to the task assigned to it and can come up with highly creative solutions to problems and issues. Sometimes these creative solutions come about because a group is more likely to make risky decisions that an individual might not undertake. This is because the group spreads responsibility for a decision to all the members and thus no single individual can be held accountable if the decision turns out to be wrong.

Taking part in a group process can be very rewarding for members of the team. Team members who have a voice in making a decision will no doubt feel better about carrying out the work that is entailed by that decision than they might doing work that is imposed on them by others. Also, the individual team member has a much better chance to "shine," to get his or her contributions and ideas not only recognized but recognized as highly significant, because a team's overall results can be more far-reaching and have greater impact than what might have otherwise been possible for the person to accomplish or contribute working alone.

Listening

Now listen to part of a lecture on the topic you just read about. Take notes if you wish.

[test taker hears:]

Now I want to tell you about what one company found when it decided that it would turn over some of its new projects to teams of people, and make the team responsible for planning the projects and getting the work done. After about six months, the company took a look at how well the teams performed.

On virtually every team, some members got almost a "free ride" … they didn't contribute much at all, but if their team did a good job, they nevertheless benefited from the recognition the team got. And what about group members who worked especially well and who provided a lot of insight on problems and issues? Well … the recognition for a job well done went to the group as a whole, no names were named. So it won't surprise you to learn that when the real contributors were asked how they felt about the group process, their attitude was just the opposite of what the reading predicts.

Another finding was that some projects just didn't move very quickly. Why? Because it took so long to reach consensus ... it took many, many meetings to build the agreement among group members about how they would move the project along. On the other hand, there were other instances where one or two people managed to become very influential over what their group did. Sometimes when those influencers said "That will never work" about an idea the group was developing, the idea was quickly dropped instead of being further discussed. And then there was another occasion when a couple influencers convinced the group that a plan of theirs was "highly creative." And even though some members tried to warn the rest of the group that the project was moving in directions that might not work, they were basically ignored by other group members. Can you guess the ending to this story? When the project failed, the blame was placed on all the members of the group.

Speaking

*You have **20 minutes** to plan and write your response. Your response will be judged on the basis of the quality of your writing and on how well your response presents the points in the lecture and their relationship to the reading passage. Typically, an effective response will be 150–225 words.*

Summarize the points made in the lecture you just heard, explaining how they cast doubt on points made in the reading.

Topic Notes

2. *Review these topic notes before reading the sample responses.*

Responses that receive scores of 4 and 5 should generally be discussing all three of the main points in the lecture and their connection to the passage (implicitly or explicitly). These points can roughly be taken as follows, though there may be some legitimate variations in interpreting and relating the information.

- Some members of a group don't work as much as others, but the rewards for success are shared equally, frustrating the true contributors.
  (This undermines the reading's claim that being part of a team is a rewarding experience, with individuals getting a chance to "shine.")
- Team work can progress very slowly, due to the time it takes to reach consensus.
  (This challenges the reading's claim that team work proceeds quickly due to the wider range of resources contributed by the individual members.)
- One or two members can dominate the others, pushing bad decisions or ignoring good suggestions (and/or resulting in blame being distributed to the rest of the group).
  (This is contrary to the claim in the passage that team work is good because all the members have a voice. It also shows the drawback of a group's willingness to take risks, touted as a good thing in the reading.)

To achieve a score of 4 or 5 there should be a clear sense of the overall relationship (i.e., that the lecture casts doubt on the claims made in the reading passage that working in groups is effective, efficient, beneficial to the members working) and some reasonable recounting of the three main points listed above. Occasionally writers will overstate or overinterpret disadvantages or advantages of group work. Responses receiving 4 for content (as opposed to language facility reasons alone) will show some minor inaccuracies in the contrast, the connections and/or the points themselves.

Responses generally cannot receive a score higher than 3 if they do not address all three points and usually will need to address two of the points of contrast. Sometimes points may be more integrated or blended together so it is important to read for overall coverage of content and not to require explicit marking of every point (though of course failure to mark points may, though not necessarily will, result in their not being presented clearly). Even responses rated 4 and 5 do not always delineate each point separately or explicitly, yet they can convey the expected content in good language.

Coverage of only one of the main points of contrast should receive no higher than a 2; i.e., it constitutes significant omission.

When assigning a score based on limitation of content, be sure to also consider whether whatever is covered is expressed in language and coherence at least commensurate with that level; that is, do not assign a score of 3 to a response that you can infer covers two points, but where you can make this inference only because you are familiar with the stimulus, not because the actual language used adequately conveys the information. Of course, accuracy and clarity of content must also be factored in per the scoring guide.

3. *Read the five benchmark responses and the annotations.*

RESPONSE

The lecturer talks about research conducted by a firm that used the group system to handle their work. He says that the theory stated in the passage was very different and somewhat inaccurate when compared to what happened for real.

First, some members got free rides. That is, some didn't work hard but gotrecognition for the success nontheless. This also indicates that people who worked hard was not given recognition they should have got. In other words, they weren't given the oppotunity to "shine". This derectly contradicts what the passage indicates.

Second, groups were slow in progress. The passage says that groups are nore responsive than individuals because of the number of people involved and their aggregated resources. However, the speaker talks about how the firm found out that groups were slower than individuals in dicision making. Groups needed more time for meetings, which are neccesary procceedures in decision making. This was another part where experience contradicted theory.

Third, influetial people might emerge, and lead the group towards glory or failure. If the influent people are going in the right direction there would be no problem. But in cases where they go in the wrong direction, there is nobody that has enough influence to counter the decision made. In other words, the group might turn into a dictatorship, with the influential party as the leader, and might be less flexible in thinking. They might become one-sided, and thus fail to succeed.

Score 5: Annotation

Once you can read past what seem to be the results of poor typing, this response does an excellent job of accurately presenting the points about the contribution and recognition of group members as well as about speed of group decisions. The final paragraph contains one noticeable error ("influent"), which is then used correctly two sentences later ("influential"), but again the point is gotten across. Overall, this is a successful response and scored within (though perhaps not at the top of) the 5-level.

RESPONSE:

The lecture that followed the paragraph on the team work in organizations, gave some negative views of the team work itself.

Firstly, though it was said in the paragraph that the whole team idea would probably be faster than the individual work, it was said in the lecture just the opposite: it could actually be a lot slower. That is because team members would sometimes take more time than needed just to reach the same conclussions, or just even to simply decide where to go from certain point to the next on.

Secondly, paragraph suggests that by doing work as a team might give you an "edge", the lecture suggests that that might also be a negative thing as well. The people who made themselves leaders in the group may just be wrong in certain decisions, or just simple thing something is so creative, when in reality it is not and it would not work, but the rest of the people would nevertheless still follow them, and end up not doing well at all. And lastly, paragraph says that everyone feels responsible for their own part, and all together they are all more effective as a team. The lecture suggests quite the opposite in this case as well. It suggests that some team members are there only for the "free ride", and they don't do much of anything to contribute, but still get the credit as a whole.

Score 4: Annotation

This response does well at attempting to interweave the points from the passage and lecture and does a good job of discussing the reaching of consensus and the issue of the "free ride." But the second body paragraph does not communicate the issue of the negative effect of people who dominate the group as clearly. The key sentence in this paragraph ("The people who made themselves leaders in the group may just be wrong in certain decisions, or just simple thing something is so creative, when in reality it is not and it would not work, but the rest of the people would nevertheless still follow them, and end up not doing well at all") represents enough of a lapse in clarity that this response is scored as a 4.

RESPONSE

The lecturer provide the opposite opinion concerning what the article offered. The team work often bring negative effet. As we all know superficially, team work and team spirits are quite popular in today's business world and also the fashionable terms. However, the lecturer find deeper and hiding results.

Firstly, the working results of team members can't be fully valued. For example, if a team member does nothing in the process of team discussion, decision making and final pratice, his or her work deliquency will not be recognized because we only emphasize team work. Also, the real excellent and creative member's work might be obliterated for the same reason.

Secondly, the team work might lose its value when team members are leading by several influential people in the group. One of the essential merits of team is to avoid the individule wrong. But one or two influential or persuasive people will make the team useless. Thirdly, team work oftem become the excuse of taking responsibillity. All in charge, nobody care.

All in all, what we should do is the fully distinguish the advantages and disadvantages of a concept or widely used method. That is to keep the common sense.

Score 3: Annotation

This response frames the issue well. The writer discusses the points about contributing ideas and about influencers in somewhat error-prone or vague and non-idiomatic language ("hiding results," "working results," and "when team members are leading by . . . influential people"). The point about influencers drops off at making the team "useless" and does not fully explain the reason that influencers create problems. The final point beginning with the word "thirdly" is not fully related to the passage and lecture, and is also unclear. This response illustrates many of typical features that can cause a response to receive the score of 3.

RESPONSE

In a company's experement, some new projects were planed and acomplished by different teams. Some teams got very good results while some teams didn't. That is to say it's not nessesary for teams to achieve more than individuals do because some team members may only contribute a little in a team for they may relying on the others to do the majority.

Another thing is the recognition for the achievement by the team is for the whole team, for everyone in the team. It's not only the dicision makers in the team feel good after successfully finishing the project, but also every member in the team.

It is also showed in the lecture that in a team with one or two leaders, sometimes good ideas from some team member are dropped and ignored while sometimes they may be highly creative. In some teams decisions were made without collecting ideas from all team members. Then it would be hard to achieve creative solutions.

For those failed projects, blames are always given to the whole team even though it's the leader or someone in the team who caught the unexpected result.

Score 2: Annotation

Although it has the appearance of a stronger response, on close reading, this response suffers from significant problems connecting ideas and misrepresenting points. For instance, the third sentence of the first paragraph seems to be getting at a point from the lecture ("some team members may contribute only a little . . . "). However, it is couched in such a way that makes it very unclear how it relates to the point of the task ("That is to say it's not necessary for teams to achieve more than individuals do because some team members may only contribute . . . "). In addition, it is not clear where the information in the second paragraph is coming from and what point the writer is trying to make. In paragraph 3 the writer tries to make a point about influencers, but again, it is not clear what information relates to what. And in the final paragraph, the phrase "caught the unexpected result" significantly obscures the real point presented in the lecture.

RESPONSE

In this lecture, the example shows only one of the group succeed the project. Why the group will succeed on this project it is because of few factor.

First of all,a group of people has a wider range of knowledge,expertise,and skills than any single individual is like to prossess, and easier to gather the information and resources to make the work effectively.and the group will willingly to trey sometihing is risky decision to make the project for interesting and suceessful. it is because all the member of the group carries the differnt responsibility for a decision, so once the decision turn wrong, no a any individual one will be blame for the whole responsiblity.

On the other way, the groups which are fail the project is because they are lay on some more influence people in the group,so even the idea is come out. Once the inflenced people say that is no good, then the process of the idea will be drop down immediately instead taking more further discussion! So the idea will not be easy to settle down for a group.

The form of the group is very important, and each of the member should be respect another and try out all the idea others had suggested,then it will develop a huge idea and the cooperate work environment for each other for effectively work!

Score 1: Annotation

The level of language used in this response is fairly low, and it is lowest in the second paragraph, which is the only reference to the lecture. Because the reader has difficulty gleaning meaning from that paragraph, the response is seen as contributing little coherent information and is therefore scored as a 1.

PRACTICE

3. *In this practice activity, there are two series of responses for you to score. There are five responses in each series. Review the Integrated Writing Task Scoring Rubric (page B-45), information about using the Scoring Rubrics (page B-30), as well as Tips for Scoring Writing Task Responses (page B-32).*

   Read the practice responses and record your score for each one BEFORE reading the next response.

Series 1

PRACTICE A

In the lecture, the professor support the opinion that to form a team is a good way to do a project. He illustrates several reasons for his point of view.

Firstly. the team can get more knowledge and experience than individual. The members of a team can cooperate each other and share their knowledge and experience. It is easy to reach a goal of a project.Each member of a team can contribute their ability to the task and express their opinion.Consequently, the team can combine these opinion together and make the project more successful.

Secondly, a team always has a same goal and members work together. However, each individual has different opnion to achieve the success. A team can divide the project into several parts and distribute each part to each person. So that the project can be achieved more efficantly.

In summary, forming a team have several advantages than individuals.

Score _____

PRACTICE B

The lecture states that team working in a given corporation did not have possitive results. This was caused by a number of reasons, one of them is the performance of the team. The performance became a problem because the team members were considered as a whole and their work was divided amongst them unequally. In the lecture, the aspect of recognition is also considered. It becomes a matter of team instead of an individual affair. This represents a problem because the work done by each member is not the same and demands a different scope. The team work, according to the lecture, has a negative impact on the speed of projects because the team s desicion making becomes complex. The agreement between every member did not happen with ease, therefore one or two became leaders and modified the other s opinion. The curse of action that got chosen was taken as the responsability of the whole team and that was unacurate at times.

On the other hand, the text states all the positive implications of team work and highlights the following< creativity, shared responsability, the ability to choose the work that each member did, individual recognition inside the team and the importance of contribution. This aspects are logical if one thinks of the theoric idea of team work, but in the practical sense, everyday life originates the ones described in the lecture. And that turns a good concept into a bad action.

Score _____

PRACTICE C

In the reading it is said that team work is relly good and makes people have more courage to take risky decisions, and it also shows other good points form team work, like having more ideas, more sources an so on.

But in the other hand, in the lecture the teacher shows the bad things about it, like having trouble on chosing the way the project will go, on concepting ideas. He also said that some people might take advantage from the group and do not work at all.This would over change some and let others free of work.

Another problem is that whem the group do a great job the group will be recognized no names will be said, this way people will not be known for what they really do.

In the reading it is said that is good to blame everyone if things go wrong, but it is bad to be recognised only by a group.And being like that people that do not work will also be recognised, and this way they will never no who is really good.

Score _____

PRACTICE D

According to the written passage, teamwork has some advantages over individual work. First, in a team, you have a wider range of knowledge and expertise. Second, members work faster and create better solutions. Third, group members are more likely to take risks because they share the reponsibility of their decisions. As a result, the members have a greater chance to shine.

However, according to an experiment conducted in a company, after six months of teamwork, they found that not much had been done because they had spent most of the time trying to reach consensus. As there are always very different opinions in a group, it is very difficult to come to an agreement about a project. In addition to that, some group members were much more influential than others and usually got things their own way, causing a bitter attitude on the other group members. Moreover, not every member of the group had contributed to the work, some had had a free ride. However, they got the same amount of recognition as the members who actually worked, and this situation also caused a feeling of frustation. So, according to the lecture, in a real-life experience, teamwork was proved to cause more problems than create solutions.

Score _____

PRACTICE E

Teamwork is sometimes good compared to individual work. Teamwork can be successful depending on how the members of the group manage how they do the project like contributing in giving ideas and deciding what they have to do first.
Sometimes working in team need more time to response to the task assigned to them as they willl argue and willl have different ideas about the task and ended in not starting doing the task . This will give them another extra time to finish or submit the job on due time.
A group of people who work together in a team sometimes do not want to listen to other member in the team. They try to be the influencer, especially those who has a stong idea about the project.

Score _____

5. *Check your scores against the trained TOEFL iBT raters' scores on page B-56.*

If your scores are different from the trained raters' scores, review the Integrated Writing Task Scoring Rubric (page B-45) and the information about the Scoring Rubrics (page B-30). Then review the benchmark responses and annotations (page B-34).

Now practice scoring five more responses in Series 2.

Series 2

PRACTICE A

The lecture provides evidence from research on team projects to counteract the benefits of team project indicated in the passage. One of the points raised is that reward for successful team work usually goes to the group as a whole and not to individuals, though some team members might not have contributed in any significant way to the achieve-ment of the team's objectives. Also, reaching group consensus is a slow process which sometimes retards the progress of teams. Furthermore, it is possible to have some team members dominating the whole process by pushing through their ideas even when such ideas are not acceptable to other members. In the end if the project does not succeed, all the members, and not the dominant few, are blamed oe suffer the consequences. These reasons cast doubt on the points made in the reading becauase the reading indicated the individual benefits of team project, such as individuals having a better chance to 'shine', and the absence of individual accountability encouraging more challenging but better decisions and bold actions. Thus whereas the reading creates the impression that team projects are all-beneficial, the lecture raises other points which express contrary views.

Score _____

PRACTICE B

In the organization, there are many advantage for group teams to work together and make some advantages to the group. Thery are some problem that individual can be better than group; however, many problem can be done better by groups. There are many different points of views in the article and lecture about group teams work.

In the article, ther are many advantage about working in group. First of all, the group member can share the ability, knowledge, and skill better than individual ;moreover, the greater number than individual make the job goes quicklier that individ-ual.

In the way group workers make a decision, it can be faster than individual because the work can be seperate and all member can help each other to make a faster decision.

In the other hand, the lecture shows that the group workers may not be able to work better and faster than in dividual because making a decision by many peo-ple take longer time than individual. The instructure shows one example about group worker problems. It is about a competition between many group workers, and it seems to be more problem during the race. Finally, some of group worker fail the work because they cannot compleate the work together.

Score _____

PRACTICE C

According to the lecture, the group work was found to have several disadvantage.

First, in a team, those who do not lively participate in the projects could enjoy free time yet gain the benefit from the team's success as the real contributors do. Even though the success is much obliged to the real contributors, they are not be praised but it is the group as a whole that enjoy the success. It is not rewarding as the reading pre-dicts.

Second, in contrast to the reading's claim that a group can work quickly, the study showed that it's the opposite. That is because it takes extra times to reach consensus and build agreement among members.

In addition, the influencer in the group can ruin the projects. The ideas rejected by the influencer are simply dropped even though other people think it is quite good. The opposite is the same story. If the influencer thinks certain idea is good, then even though other people warn that it might not work, the idea will be the winner.

   The results are even worse. It the projects led by the influencer fails, it's all the members who are blamed.

Score _____

PRACTICE D

the lecture and passage talk their relationship in the team and who the comfort . the decision that people with knowledge take in the team and solution risky decisions. the members that form part of team help the others members

Score _____

PRACTICE E

The lecture and the paragraph are completely contradictory. First of all, the lecture says that the work of the group is going to be recognized in a hole, not individually, giving no space for this last. Second, the lecture says that the work is going to take more time once that the group is going to take more discussions and take time to decide how are they going to proceed within the group work. Besides that the one who leads the group has the power, somehow, to see if the discussion is going to proceed or if it's going to be hiden, and, in this way, make his/her personal desire kept in front of the others. We can also percept that as a group there will be someones who's going to carry the group on their back and trere'll be others who'll be static without doing even a single thing. By these points of view we can see that there advantages and disadvantages in group working.

Score _____

6. *Check your scores against the trained TOEFL iBT raters' scores on page B-56.*

If your scores are different from the trained raters' scores, review the Integrated Writing Task Scoring Rubric (page B-45) and the information about the Scoring Rubrics (page B-30). Then review the benchmark responses and annotations (page B-34).

TRAINED TOEFL iBT RATERS' SCORES FOR PRACTICE SETS 3 AND 4 (WRITING)

The scores below were assigned by trained raters in a pilot test of the TOEFL iBT given to a representative sample of TOEFL test takers. Two raters scored each response and assigned the same score to the responses.

INDEPENDENT WRITING

Series 1, page B-38	**Series 2**, page B-41
PRACTICE A: 4	PRACTICE A: 3
PRACTICE B: 2	PRACTICE B: 4
PRACTICE C: 1	PRACTICE C: 1
PRACTICE D: 5	PRACTICE D: 2
PRACTICE E: 3	PRACTICE E: 5

INTEGRATED WRITING

Series 1, page B-51	**Series 2**, page B-53
PRACTICE A: 1	PRACTICE A: 5
PRACTICE B: 4	PRACTICE B: 2
PRACTICE C: 3	PRACTICE C: 4
PRACTICE D: 5	PRACTICE D: 1
PRACTICE E: 2	PRACTICE E: 3

MORE ABOUT PERFORMANCE FEATURES OF WRITING TASK RESPONSES

When scoring, you should associate certain performance features listed in the Writing Task Scoring Rubrics with certain score levels. For this reason, it is important to understand the definitions of these features and how they apply to a writing task.

1. Organization

Organization traditionally refers to the overall approach a writer uses to present information. Writers usually try to help the reader understand how the larger ideas are connected using such devices as paragraph breaks, topic sentences, transitional sentences and phrases, and transition words[1] and also sometimes by writing introductory paragraphs that tell the reader what to expect in the rest of the piece of writing. You as a rater, however, should not be consciously looking for these features when you are evaluating the quality of writing. If the writer has done a good job with organization, you will be able to consistently follow and understand what your student's major ideas are and how they are related. You might even be able to predict what your student will

---

[1]See Appendices A and B in this Teacher's Manual for lists of signal words and phrases, and transition words and phrases.

talk about next. But if the writing has problems of organization, you *will* notice something wrong—problems that are discussed in other definitions here, problems of *coherence,* of *connection,* and of *progression.* Poor organization in an Integrated Task response could even lead you to judge that the writer has communicated *inaccurate* information because some information may be improperly associated with other information.

2. Coherence

When writing is coherent, you can consistently understand or easily make the *connections among ideas* that the writer intends. In writing that is said to be *incoherent,* the reader has severe difficulty inferring connections that the writer intends or perhaps cannot infer meaning at all. Also at the sentence level, unrecognizable grammatical structures or unmeaningful combinations of words often are perceived as incoherent. In writing that has some problems of coherence, usually you as the reader have to try to guess at meaning or connection that the writer intends; for example, logical reasoning or knowledge or beliefs. These ideas or connections are perhaps in the mind of the writer but they are not stated in the response and thus they are not obviously understood by you.

3. Unity, Progression, and Redundancy

These terms are used only in the Independent Writing Task Scoring Rubrics. *Unity* refers to the central content of the essay. A writer who keeps the response "unified" keeps the presentation *focused* on the central point and does not "wander off" into points that do not support or explain the main idea or *progression* of ideas being discussed. Don't just assume that paragraphs always advance the progression of ideas: a writer might begin three paragraphs of support with "First," "Second," "Third," but if the third point is really a *digression* on the second point and not centrally related to the *main purpose* of the writing (sometimes this is called the writer's *thesis*), then the writing does not display unity. If the third point or any point is really a restatement of something already presented, it is *redundant* and does not contribute to the progression of ideas.

4. Development/Elaboration

Development refers to the amount and kinds of support presented. Support can come in the form of explanation, examples, and details that the writer produces from knowledge and experience. In the Independent Writing Task, the support is generated and developed by the writer (see also *specificity*) and the more said about each piece of support, the more *elaborated* it is. In the Integrated Writing Task, the information the writer needs comes from the reading passage and the lecture. In this task, the writer needs to present the information that is requested by the question. One of the main distinctions between a 4 and a 5 level response in the rubric is that support for the key ideas and supporting points at the 4 level are not as *fully* elaborated as they are at the 5 level. At the lower levels, in the Independent Writing Task, a 2-level response may have only "limited" development; in the Integrated Writing Task, you might judge a response a 2 level because the elaboration of key points is "significantly" incomplete.

5. Specificity

Sometimes development is also linked with the terms *specificity* or development of *specifics*. Most often, when development proceeds with specificity, there are more detailed stretches of explanations and examples to support major ideas. Sometimes specificity is associated with giving "concrete" details. The opposite of specificity is *generality* or sometimes general level of abstraction. Writers who develop entire essays at a very general level are likely not to have as much overall information to develop and are not as likely to demonstrate good progression because it is difficult to sustain elaboration and explanation without specificity.

6. Responsiveness/Effective response/Completeness/Accuracy/Inaccuracy

A piece of writing that directly does what the question asks is said to be *responsive* to the task. In Independent Writing, if an essay does not at all address the topic and task, it is said to be off-topic. If it is not clear whether the writer is responding to the task, you should assign a 1 for "questionable responsiveness." An effective response to the Independent Writing Task not only is responsive but also uses appropriate elaboration that provides clear, relevant support of the writer's point of view. In the Integrated Writing Task, one of your main judgments will be how *complete* and how *accurate* the information is that the writer presents. For degrees of completeness, you will judge how much key information has been included and how much has been left out. You judge degrees of inaccuracy according to how severely the information conveyed differs from what was actually stated or implied in the lecture and reading passage.

7. Meaning—general

There are many ways to look at *meaning* in the context of writing. The most common kind of "meaning" has to do with the ideas of the writer, the thoughts that the writer is trying to express; these are sometimes called the writer's *intention*. When you read a piece of writing, especially an essay whose content comes primarily from the thoughts and experience and opinions of your student, you are trying to get meaning from the essay. As you read, you are trying to understand the words and phrases and sentences—the ideas that are stated—and you are also trying to understand the connections between these that the writer is making through language. And at the same time, you are also trying to *infer* ideas and connections that you believe the writer wants or expects you to understand. When all goes well, the writer writes—conveying intentions in words, sentences, paragraphs, the essay as whole—and the reader reads, forming an "interpretation" or "understanding" that matches what the writer intended the reader to understand.

What can go wrong? First, writers may not have clearly formulated the ideas they want to express. If this is so, then it is likely that you as the reader will perceive part or all of the writing as at least *unclear, unconnected,* or *"digressive,"* and at the extreme, *incoherent* or *unintelligible*. Second, writers may have reasonably clear ideas they want to express, but they may *lack facility* (overall or in specific areas)—they may not have or they do not know how to use effectively the range of vocabulary and expressions in English to make their ideas understood. In such cases, you as the reader may perceive some of the meaning and connections to be *unclear* or *imprecise* or *vague,* or at a more severe level, you will not be able to derive meaning. If you have difficulty deriving meaning because of the language, it may be because the language use has *obscured* the meaning. A third way in which meaning may not seem clear may have to do with *you* having been distracted or inattentive. If you believe this is possible, you should reread to see if your difficulty of interpretation had to do with your reading behavior at the moment or had to do with something your student should learn to do better.

8. Meaning—Integrated Tasks

In the case of the Integrated Writing Task, you need to take multiple perspectives on the concept of "meaning." Your students will be deriving meaning from the reading passage and the lecture. This is their comprehended meaning—the "understanding" or "interpretation" that your students have arrived at. There is probably no one final interpretation that an individual makes once and for all time. Some earlier understandings may change as students are asked to recall or reread and then write about what they have previously understood. In the TOEFL iBT Integrated Writing Tasks, your students are asked to do their best to communicate in writing *their* current understandings in response to the question asked about the reading and the lecture. The Key Points or Topic Notes are intended to represent for you the understandings or interpretations that *a competent reader or listener of English* would derive from the lecture and passage and then put forth as answers to the questions. In judging your students' responses, you will really be doing two things. You will first be interpreting *their language* to try to understand *their interpretations* of what they believe they are supposed to comprehend and then present in writing. After you have judged *their interpretations,* you then evaluate how well what they have conveyed *matches* the "ideal" information suggested as a full or ample response to the question. To say it again, it is important to see this as a two-stage process: First, you are interpreting the meaning that your students' language conveys and immediately after that you are comparing your students' interpretations with the interpretation provided in the Key Points. As you are dealing with the first stage, interpreting the student's meaning from the student's language, you should read in the same way you read the independent writing—almost as if you don't know what the student intends. So here you have to deal with issues of language facility and of imprecise formulation of ideas. Then as a separate mental act, you evaluate the accuracy and degree of the match with the content coverage in the Key Points or Topic Notes.

9. Language facility/Word choice/Syntactic variety/Range of vocabulary

Writers who have well thought-out and complex *intentions* to express can only communicate the complexity and intricacies of these intentions by using the great number and range of structures *(syntactic variety),* words *(range of vocabulary),* and expressions available in English and by using these in appropriate contexts. The term *language facility* refers to the overall effective use of English to communicate complex ideas. Writers who have not yet acquired this facility, or who are not able to use the knowledge they have learned effectively, are more limited in what they are able to express to a reader. You know a writer has *consistent facility* in language use when you are able to read and, without effort, fully understand and appreciate sustained presentation of complex ideas. For the Integrated Writing Task, writers demonstrate facility by making effective use of structures and choosing appropriate words to accurately and efficiently convey the information that responds to the question.

10. Inconsistent facility/Infacility/Error in structure/Word choice error/Error in language use

These terms all apply to problems in the use of English that a reader would certainly notice. Structure errors mean the sentence does not follow the grammatical rules of English. Some structure errors, if they occur infrequently in writing, are considered minor—almost as "oversights" by the writer that could be easily corrected (and indeed often are easily corrected in the mind of the reader, with almost no notice). Similarly, using a "non-word" but possible-looking word such as "independency" instead of the accurate word choice "independence" might be considered minor if it occurs in a longer stretch of otherwise accurate language use. Errors become more noticeable as they move away from or violate well-defined grammatical patterns; for example, getting the incorrect part of speech in a phrase like "becomes independence" for "becomes independent." Even more severely judged might be a phrase such as "They prefer to be depended on their parents" (even though a student may have heard at some point "be dependent on," and in a student's *speech*, this sentence might *sound* fully comprehensible and grammatical). In evaluating language, you are making a judgment not merely about how many errors or misexpressions are present, but also about the effect these errors or expressions have on the reader's being able to understand; the phrase "be depended on" would probably strike an ordinary reader of English as a strange and possibly close-to-meaningless expression. So in judging language use, the greater the numbers of structure errors and especially the greater the number of expressions and grammatical patterns that fail to convey meaning or obscure meaning or communicate a meaning different from the one intended, the more you will rate the writer as having *inconsistent facility* or even *consistent infacility* in English.

11. Idiomatic/Unidiomatic language/Idiomaticity

As used here, idiomatic language and idiomaticity do *not* refer to "idioms," that is, expressions whose meaning cannot be determined by knowing the meaning of the parts. The scoring rubrics use these terms to describe language—words, phrases, and structures — that is grammatical and meaningful but that is not to be used by a native speaker of English in the context the writer has used them. A simple example would be an expression such as "They had hunger," where the idiomatic way to express this concept would be "They were hungry." Another example is that in English one says "I come from" or "I am from" to indicate country of birth or origin; someone who used the expression "I came from . . ." would be judged as conveying information somewhat unidiomatically. Of course, what is idiomatic is something that can vary slightly according to the variety of native English speakers.

12. Connection

From the writer's point of view, *connection* refers both to how the writer intends for ideas to be related to each other and to what the writer actually does in language (connective words and phrases, placement of sentences next to each other, topic sentences, etc.) to direct the reader to understand the relationship among the ideas. From the reader's point of view, connection is how clearly the reader actually understands relationships or the degree of difficulty the reader has in understanding the relationships between and among ideas. Sometimes you can have difficulty understanding connections because the writer has failed to supply certain key unstated information or background information. Sometimes the writer has failed to use enough language to make the connections explicit enough for you. Or sometimes you may have difficulty understanding because your students aren't clear in their own minds what kinds of connections among ideas they intend to make.

13. Clarity/Precision/Precise/Imprecision/Imprecise

If you perceive language use and overall presentation of information to be *clear*, then you feel you understand exactly what the writer wants to convey. If you are unsure exactly what the writer is trying to convey or how the writer intends for you to relate certain information to other information, then the writer is displaying *lack of clarity*. In the Integrated Tasks, you are making judgments not only about the presence or absence of information the writer is expected to write about (completeness) but also the quality of the information that is presented. How well the writer presents information in language and how well the writer connects the information will all go into your judgment of how clearly and how precisely the writer has represented the Key Points or Topic Notes.

Signal Words and Phrases

Knowing the signal words and phrases below can help listeners understand the organization of lectures, conversations, and interviews. Using signal words in spoken responses helps listeners understand and follow the response.

"For example" is a very common signal phrase that speakers use to introduce an example. Other common signals include:	"There are three reasons why …" "First … Second … Third …" "What I want to talk about is …"	"And most important, …" "A major development …" "Why it was so important …"
An instructor may signal supporting details with phrases such as:	"On the other hand …" "Last time …" "On the contrary …" "For example, …" "Just like …" "Similarly, …" "In contrast, …" "Also, …"	"So …" "And in fact, …" "Further, …" "A term for …" "Furthermore, …" "As an example, …" "For instance, …" "But …"
An instructor may signal conclusion or summary with:	"Therefore, …" "In conclusion, …" "In other words, …" "As a result, …"	"Finally, …" "In summary, …" "From this we see that …"
A speaker may signal important information very directly with:	"Now this is important …" "The thing about …"	"Remember that …" "The important idea is that …"

Adapted from *TOEFL® iBT Tips.* Copyright © 2005 by Educational Testing Service. Used with permission.

Transition Words and Phrases

Knowing the words and phrases below is useful for understanding transitions in news articles, academic texts, essays, and stories. Using transition words and phrases in written responses can help readers understand the organization of the writing and the connection between ideas.

PURPOSE	
Sequence	again, also, and, and then, finally, first, second, third, next, still, too, and so forth, afterward, subsequently, finally, consequently, previously, before this, simultaneously, concurrently
To add	besides, equally important, finally, further, furthermore, nor, lastly, what's more, moreover, in addition
To prove	because, for since, for the same reason, obviously, evidently, furthermore, moreover, besides, indeed, in fact, in addition, in any case, that is
To compare and contrast	whereas, but, yet, on the other hand, however, nevertheless, on the contrary, by comparison, where compared to, up against, balanced against, vis a vis, but, although, conversely, meanwhile, after all, in contrast, although this may be true, still, though, yet, despite, as opposed to
Time	immediately, thereafter, soon, after a few hours, finally, then, later, previously, formerly, first (second, etc.), next, and then, as long as, as soon as
Cause-and-effect	as a result, because, consequently, for this purpose, so, then, therefore, to this end
Emphasis	definitely, extremely, obviously, in fact, indeed, in any case, absolutely, positively, naturally, surprisingly, always, forever, perennially, eternally, never, emphatically, unquestionably, without a doubt, certainly, undeniably, without reservation
Exception	yet, still, however, nevertheless, in spite of, despite, of course, once in a while, sometimes
Examples	for example, for instance, in this case, in another case, on this occasion, in this situation, take the case of, to demonstrate, to illustrate, as an illustration, to illustrate, such as
To summarize and conclude	in brief, on the whole, summing up, to conclude, in conclusion, as I have shown, hence, therefore, accordingly, thus, as a result, consequently, as has been noted, as we have seen

CD TRACKING LIST

Notes

Notes

Notes

Notes

Notes

Notes

Notes

Notes

Notes

Notes